GETTING STARTED IN THE UNDERGROUND ECONOMY

ADAM CASH

Loompanics Unlimited
Port Townsend, Washington

Getting Started In The Underground Economy
© 1987 by Loompanics Unlimited

Published by:
Loompanics Unlimited
PO Box 1197
Port Townsend, WA 98368
Loompanics Unlimited is a division of Loompanics Enterprises, Inc.

ISBN 01-915179-46-6
Library of Congress Catalog Card Number 86-82955

Contents

"*There is one difference between a tax collector and a taxidermist — the taxidermist leaves the hide.*"
—**Mortimer Caplan, Director of the Bureau of Internal Revenue, 1963**

1

Introduction

GUERRILLA CAPITALISM and *HOW TO DO BUSINESS "OFF THE BOOKS"* gave you valuable information on how to earn money without paying taxes on it. This third volume will give you more of the same, but with a few additional features:

■ It will show you some of the ways in which the government wastes your hard-earned tax money and then asks you for more.

■ It will show you how to save more of the money you do earn, both on direct expenditures and on taxes.

■ It will show you how to take some little-noted and little-used deductions on your income tax return.

Obviously, not all of these methods will be for everyone. No single individual could use all of them, at least not all at once. However, there is a wide enough variety presented here to give you some choices.

This is basically a self-improvement book. But unlike many other entries in this genre, it does not pretend to provide any "secret" formula for quick and easy riches. There is no easy way to become rich, except by inheritance, and few of us are lucky enough to enjoy that. You are not likely to become rich, and certainly not by reading a book.

1

However, by reading *this* book, and acting upon the information that is relevant to your needs, you *can* improve your situation. You still won't be rich, but you will be better off than before.

Do you want to be more fiscally fit? If you do, then read on.

2

Taxes and Government Waste

Government spending is out of control. In 1948, federal, state and local spending amounted to $55 billion. By 1985, it totaled a trillion and a half dollars, 27 times more than in 1948.

Much of this skyrocketing spending, especially on the federal level, has been financed through borrowing, with the result that the national debt is now over $2 trillion. And that's just what the government has *already* borrowed. It doesn't include the unfunded future obligations the government has assumed for various programs and projects. According to the National Taxpayers Union, total federal obligations actually amount to more than $13 trillion.[1]

But even the official debt is so large that interest payments alone now make up about an eighth of the federal budget.[2] And the NTU projects that if current deficit trends continue, by 1990 interest payments on the debt will account for 28% of the budget.[3] With the government this deep in debt, is there any way it will ever be able to climb back out of the hole?

In any case, growing government spending has meant, not just growing deficits, but growing taxes too. According to the conservative calculations of Dr. Gary North, the percentage of average family income taken by federal, state and local taxes increased from 14% in 1947 to 22.2% in 1982.[4] But a less conservative estimate of the current tax burden is given by William R. Kennedy, Jr. "Indeed," writes Kennedy, "when Middle Americans add up their federal income tax, state income tax, Social Security tax (with employer's contribution), as well as sales, property, and other 'item' taxes, more than 50 percent of their income has most likely disappeared into the hands of bureaucrats."[5]

Whatever the precise percentage, the tax burden on Americans is higher than ever, despite the "Reagan Revolution." What about the famous Reagan tax cuts of 1981? As Dr. Gary North says, "Yes, some cuts in federal income tax were passed in 1981. Meanwhile, state and local governments increased their tax load in order to catch all of the 'rebates' from the federal government. Then, in 1982, the *largest tax increase in American history* was approved. However, it wasn't called raising taxes. It was called *saving Social Security*. Now, thanks to those TEFRA increases, Social Security is the largest single tax the American worker pays. (There's no 'dependents deduction' or any kind of deduction of FICA taxes.) And it's going to go higher; the increases are already on the books."[6]

If taxes are increasing because of increasing spending, then what about that spending? Is it all necessary? Or is the government wasting taxpayers' dollars?

Is the Pope Catholic? Do wild bears shit in the woods? However much people of different political persuasions disagree about which parts of the budget constitute waste, hardly anyone will deny that the government throws money around like a drunken sailor with only one weekend left to live.

For some years, Senator William Proxmire has been identifying instances of wasteful spending and giving his "Golden Fleece" award for particularly outrageous examples of such waste. Much of his recent book, *The Fleecing of America*, is devoted to criticizing federally funded research. Among the examples included: an HEW project to teach

4

college students to watch TV, a study of how long it takes to cook hash and fry eggs, and a study of why prisoners want to escape from jail.[7]

The Grace Commission, which spent 18 months evaluating the federal bureaucracy, concluded that about $140 billion dollars a year could be saved by eliminating waste and inefficiency, without even abolishing any major program.[8] (And plausible arguments have been made that many such major programs are simply a waste of taxpayers' money.)

The upshot of all this is that taxpayers are not getting their money's worth. Thus, for example, "...the Grace Commission points out that '100 percent of what is collected' in personal income taxes 'is absorbed solely by interest on the federal debt and by federal government contributions to transfer payments. In other words, all individual income tax revenues are gone before one nickel is spent on the services which taxpayers expect from their government."[9] And, according to the NTU, as a result of government spending and taxing policies, an average American family is $2,893 poorer than it was ten years ago.[10]

No wonder Americans are increasingly seeking to avoid paying taxes and to keep what they earn. No wonder the underground economy is growing to such an extent that the tax collectors have become seriously concerned. And as long as the government continues to pursue its present preposterous policies, individuals will no doubt continue to seek means of protecting themselves from the effects of those policies.

NOTES

1. "NTU Releases Taxpayer Liability Figures," *Dollars & Sense*, March 1986, p. 5.

2. "The Budget Revolution That Wasn't," by Doug Bandow, *Reason*, May 1985, p. 41.

3. "NTU Goes to Court on Behalf of Nation's Children," *Dollars & Sense*, March 1986, p. 4.

4. *Twelve Deadly Negatrends*, by Dr. Gary North, Fort Worth, TX, American Bureau of Economic Research, 1985, pp. 65-66.

5. *A Taxpayer Survey of the Grace Commision Report,* by William R. Kennedy, Jr. and Robert W. Lee, Ottawa, IL, Green Hill Publishers, 1984, p. 2.

6. *Twelve Deadly Negatrends*, by Dr. Gary North, pp. 69-70.

7. "Inside the Mind of a Big-Time Spender," by James L. Payne, *Reason*, July 1986, p. 43.

8. *A Taxpayer Survey of the Grace Commission Report*, by William R. Kennedy, Jr. and Robert W. Lee, p. 1.

9. *Ibid.*, pp. 21-22.

10. National Taxpayers Union, 325 Pennsylvania Avenue, S.E., Washington, D.C. 20003.

3

The Myth of a Steady Job

Most of us have believed, at one time or another, that the way to economic security is through getting a steady job with a large company, and enjoying the benefits of a regular paycheck with many fringe benefits, including retirement plans. We're indoctrinated into this fallacy in school and by our parents, as well as by propaganda in the media.

The reality is quite different. While there still are some people who "hire on at 18, retire at 65," they are a tiny minority. A steady career with a large company, despite the myth, is usually neither rewarding nor secure.

Anyone who hasn't been asleep during the last ten years has seen the news of one large, "respectable" company after another either going bankrupt or laying off many employees. The auto industry, once considered the mainstay of the American economy, is a perfect example of both. Technological obsolescence, foreign competition, and an unhealthy economy can cause a disaster for the employee of a large company.

When a large company either fails completely or has a massive layoff, the propects of the laid-off employee are especially bleak, because he'll face intense competition from many other former employees in seeking a new job in that area. When several thousands are suddenly out of work, they saturate the market, and the individual will either be out of work for a long time or have to take a job that pays much less, because a mass layoff suddenly makes it a "buyer's market." Prospective employers know that they have many desperate applicants for every opening they offer, and they can be ruthless in setting wages.

The security the individual seeks by working for a large company just isn't there. A pension plan seems appealing on paper, but most of them require a certain period on the job before the employee is "vested," that is, entitled to the benefits. If he's laid off before then, he simply gets back what he paid into it, and he's literally out on the street.

Executives of many large companies, especially the ones which have regular layoffs, cynically set the "vesting" period just long enough so that the majority of the employees will be caught in a layoff before the time is up, which enables the company to offer very appealing paper benefits without having to pay off on them for most employees. Many excellent examples of this practice occur in the "defense" industries, where production follows the awarding of government contracts and mass layoffs come at the end of the contracts.

The minority who manage to hold on to their jobs through the recurrent storms of layoffs find themselves in other binds. Most of us have heard the term "wage slave," and know what it means. An employee who feels trapped, who works for years at an unrewarding job, is a wage slave. He counts the days to retirement, knowing that if he leaves his employment he'll lose his pension. This is a device used by employers who want to keep some of their employees without offering additional pay in proportion to their skill and experience.

The long-term employee is more often victimized than rewarded. Managers, instead of seeing them as exceptionally loyal workers, view them as dull plodders who lack the initiative to seek anything better. Accordingly, they hold back pay increases, feeling that the employee is powerless or too weak-willed to protest in the most effective manner possible: by finding another job.

In practice, the employee who wants better pay and benefits will usually find it by seeking another job, not within his present one. This is one important reason why there's so much turnover in the job market.

THE SEARCH FOR SECURITY

The key word is *diversification*, a term often used in business. A large company tries not to put all its eggs in one basket, and seeks to avoid the threats of overwhelming competition and technological obsolescence by entering different areas. Similarly, an employee can find security more quickly and effectively by following the same plan.

The single-paycheck employee can, if he loses his job, be out in the cold very quickly and very suddenly. One with several sources of income stands to lose only part of it at one time. This is why many people hold more than one job, or keep portfolios of stocks and bonds. It's still possible, but extremely unlikely, to be wiped out all at once when there are multiple incomes. Diversification pays off!

It's a simple and obvious idea, but one book presents it as a "secret."[1] It's not a secret at all, but a simple principle followed by businessmen and employees alike.

This is why many people "moonlight," not just for the extra income. In one important sense, moonlighting above-ground, which means paying extra taxes, is still beneficial because it brings extra security. A part-time job is valuable when the employee's company suddenly lays him off. It can hold things together awhile, and can even work into a full-time job if the opportunity and timing are right.

The laid-off employee with a sideline, something unconnected with his regular work, finds that with extra time on his hands, he can expand his business to earn more money, and with persistence and a little luck can even make it his main income.

NOTES

1. *555 Ways To Earn Extra Money,* Jay Conrad Levinson, New York, Holt, Rinehart, and Winston, 1982, p. 13.

4

Some Underground Economy People

Tommy works as a printer, and is exceptionally good at his trade. A printing equipment service technician suggested to him that he pick up extra money by working as a consultant, pointing out that many print shops had problems with their equipment, techniques, and hired help, and expert advice could save an owner much more than the fee he'd pay for it. Tommy's first client had a technical problem that neither he nor his employees could master. Tommy solved the problem for him, spending several hours at the client's facility, and charging him three times his normal hourly rate. This client paid Tommy by check, but referred him to others, who were willing to go along with Tommy's proposal of a discount in return for cash. One client, sympathetic to Tommy's goal, paid him by check to provide a deduction for his own tax return, but cashed the check for Tommy, to break the paperwork trail.

David always had a green thumb, even as a child. As an adolescent, he mowed lawns. As an adult, he spent fifteen frustrating years working at dull, unrewarding jobs before he found himself. He started his own landscaping service, accepting commercial clients but concentrating on homeowners, who more often pay in cash. He declares less income than he actually makes, and is careful to keep his deductions down to fit the profile of his type of business, even throwing away legitimate receipts to avoid giving the impression of ordering too many supplies for the declared volume of business.

Ed, a technical writer for a major electronics company, owns a word processor which he uses for his above-ground work and for writing novels, his real love. He recently sold his first novel, but despite his heavy schedule finds time to write resumes for people in his plant who need them for job-seeking. As there's a high turn-over, he has a constant source of clients. His word processor enables him to use a time-saving method to turn out resumes for his clients. He has several standard forms recorded on a disk, each with the framework for words and blank spaces for names, dates, and other particular information. When he gets a job he brings the most suitable one up on his screen and fills in the blanks. This takes very little time, compared to typing it from scratch, and within a few minutes he has a high-grade printout. He has a letter-quality printer that uses carbon ribbons, which makes originals of excellent quality, suitable for offset reproduction at a quick-print shop. He offers his clients a choice of services, from just making up a resume to a complete package. He is friendly with a quick-printer near his home, and if the client buys the whole package he'll have the quick-printer turn out the number of copies ordered, some even with the client's photograph, which he sells to the client at a markup.

Samantha is a fourteen-year-old who is very mature for her age, and has a reputation for reliability among her neighbors, who have known her since her family moved in ten years ago. She baby-sits almost every night of the week, collecting in cash. She doesn't have a Social Security number yet, which makes her invisible to the IRS. At a client's house, she's careful not to abuse her trust, and does not invite boyfriends over or tie up the telephone. After putting her charges to bed, she does her homework, and the sight of her poring over her studies when the parents come home enhances her image. She has no trouble staying "booked," and stashes most of her income in her parents' savings account, rather than opening one of her own. Her father, a lawyer, advised her to use this method to keep her income untraceable, and willingly pays the tax on the interest her savings earn.

John is a backyard mechanic, not employed in the field, but very handy with small tools and skilled enough to do his own automotive repairs and maintenance. In fact, his hobby is cars, and he earns extra money by buying broken-down old clunkers and restoring them to almost-new condition. This takes a lot of hours, but as it is his hobby, he doesn't mind. Every year or two, he finishes a restoration and sells it for several thousand dollars. This gives him some extra tax-free income. Although his buyers always pay by check, and he cannot launder such large checks, he feels safe in depositing the checks in his personal account, because he holds a regular job as an aircraft assembler, and his station in life and the tax picture the IRS has of him is so conventional as not to attract attention. He has never been audited.

Amy is a good-looking co-ed who earns money by selling sandwiches to office workers. With her miniskirt, attractive smile, and a basket full of assorted sandwiches, she makes the rounds in an office building just before lunchtime every day, selling her homemade sandwiches to those who are too busy, or too lazy, to leave their desks. She does well for several reasons. She has an attractive body and personality. People like her. She offers good food, always fresh and attractively prepared, and her portions are generous. She has the connivance of both company executives and the management of the building. They let her make her rounds, without even asking for a percentage of her sales, because she told them outright that she is a student working her way through college, which is true. She is able to earn a good rate of profit because the building she works is in mid-town Manhattan, where there is a huge lunch-time crowd, and the restaurants have long waiting lines, as do many sandwich shops. They charge what the traffic will bear. Amy is able to charge the same price, but offers sandwiches which are as good or better, and the convenience of delivery right to the customer's desk. She is always slightly overstocked, and what she doesn't sell she offers to building maintenance men and others as she leaves, building good will at no additional cost.

Dick works as an airport security police officer, and on his days off he installs burglar alarms. He's a partner in a security business, covering alarms, armored automobiles, special weapons, and other defensive paraphernalia, and thus can't run his sideline completely underground. However, he services both businesses and private homes, which gives him the opportunity of offering the private homeowner a discount for cash. This lets him "skim" a lot of money on his own accounts, with his partner's knowledge and consent. Another sideline he runs is pure installation. He lets the customer choose and buy the alarm system he wants, through his firm or another, and Dick does the installation. This way, there's no record of his buying any components, and he gets away cleanly if the customer pays cash. This is an important point, as an IRS audit can reveal the purchase his company made, and the auditor can infer the number of installations from the number of components.

As a boy, Frank learned the shoe repair business, working in his father's shop. He decided not to enter the field, instead working as a telephone installer. This brings him into contact with many people, especially fellow employees who need repairs on their expensive work boots. He does this as a sideline, charging about one-third the price that a shoe repair shop does, and has enough cash customers to fill many of his off-duty hours.

Bud used to be an upholsterer until he became an electronics technician for a large manufacturing company. He still operates a private practice, during the evenings and on weekends. He earns more per hour, and gets to keep it all. His medical plan, retirement, etc., are all paid for by his regular employer, which enables him to enjoy the best of both worlds.

Eric is a young man with excellent eyesight, and enviable skill with a rifle. He lives in a rural area, and spends his weekends outdoors. Some of this earns him money. Local farmers have trouble with predators, such as crows, field mice, and coyotes. Eric offers to rid their farms of predators, and has the farmers pay him a fixed fee per head. He uses a scope-sighted .22 rifle, and his skill is such that he has made hundred-yard kills. At one dollar each, it pays for more than the cost of his ammunition.

Maryann is a "bag lady." She earns her subsistence by picking through other peoples' garbage. She often finds items which she can re-sell to earn money for food. She even finds food, as some people throw out canned goods. Her clothing is all "recycled," and some of it is of excellent quality, having been thrown out by wealthy purchasers because it was no longer in style.

Max is a retired police officer. He supplements his generous pension by working in the broad field known as "private investigation." His method of operation is free-lance, and he's basically self-employed. He does accident investigation for an agency operated by a friend of his, another retiree. He spends most of his time, however, as a process server. His list of clients includes most of the prominent lawyers in his city, and he has no shortage of business. There's a lot of pressure in this sort of work. Typically, a lawyer will hand him a sheaf of summonses and tell him that he must serve them all that day, as the trial begins the following day. He gets paid by the piece, and how much effort he needs to serve the paper depends on his skill, and his luck. Because his workload is so heavy, he can be very efficient in his effort. With many papers to serve, he doesn't drive very far between the addresses, although call-backs to catch the people who were not at home are a constant annoyance. Although he collects by check, his friend with the detective agency helps him launder a part of his collections. He passes off some checks at his regular gas station, where the owner, a long-time friend, is cooperative.

5

What Do YOU Want?

What are your needs? What are your wants? Some people really don't earn enough to make ends meet, and welcome the chance to earn extra money, not necessarily in the underground economy, but any way they can, even if they have to pay extra taxes on the extra income.

Others resist paying taxes because of a profound conviction that the government wastes their money. These people often hold full-time jobs and pay taxes on their incomes, but want to earn extra tax-free money.

Some want "pin money," or "mad money," to buy luxuries that they could not otherwise afford.

Some want to develop a skill or a business to supplement retirement income. This need not be something that is done only after retirement, as it's best to acquire a resource before the actual need for it.[1]

Others, with a hard-core survivalist orientation, feel that the economy will sooner or later crash, and they want a way of earning a living that is inflation- or depression-proof. These may also seek to put away supplies for survival. These can range from freeze-dried foods through silver coins to guns and ammunition.[2]

Yet others simply resent paying taxes, and want to be able to keep all of what they earn.

There are other motives, and other needs, and one person can have two or more reasons at the same time. The main point is to understand *your* motives and needs, and to assign priorities.

Are you interested in extra income, regardless of whether or not you have to pay taxes on it?

Do you distrust the Social Security system, so that you feel the need to assure your retirement income?

Are you apprehensive about the economy, so that you feel you need to provide for surviving economic collapse?

Do you object to paying taxes, or feel that you're being tapped for more than your share? Are you willing to take risks to avoid taxes? If so, how big?

Do you just like to "get away with something," as many of us faced with a crushing economic situation and an oppressive society do?

Are you greedy, or do you like to conspicuously show off what you own?

Only you can answer these questions. Answer them honestly, because only accurate answers will enable you to plan to meet your needs. Be aware of your weaknesses, such as greed or the need to show off, because these can be dangerous liabilities if you enter the underground economy.

WHAT LEVEL FOR YOU?

Rather than try to promote or dictate a certain inflexible technique of earning money in the underground economy, I'll try to point out the possibilities.

While the facts about the economy are fairly clear, those about Guerrilla Capitalists are not. This is because people vary so much in skills and personalities. They vary in willingness to change their lifestyles, and willingness to take risks. Let's examine some of the checkpoints along the road to the underground. Identifying these different levels of involvement will enable you to select what best suits your skills, personality, and life situation.

LEVEL I: Dipping your toes into the water.

This basically means exploiting the opportunities in your regular occupation, something which many people are doing already. If you're self-employed, you have the chance to skim off some of the receipts without declaring them on your tax return. A doctor, for example, still gets paid in cash occasionally, and if he's discreet, he can pocket some of it without making waves, or even ripples. A plumber also gets cash jobs, as does a repairman, lawn care specialist, etc.

There are, however, two main points to keep in mind in this effort.

First, don't skim so much that it shows conspicuously. If you deprive your business of too much visible income, the experienced examiners at the IRS may note the imbalance, and wonder how you can afford to incur so many business expenses, or occupy such a large building, with so little income. The corollary to this is to watch your deductible expenses, and not deduct more than is appropriate for the income you declare.

Tax examiners have carefully worked out guidelines that tell them what the normal proportions of expenses are in relation to income. From examining many tax returns, they've worked out averages for almost every sort of deduction. For example, they have computed what proportion of income goes for church contributions in different income brackets. They know what the average figure is for supplies in various types of businesses. If your tax return seems out of proportion, it will suggest to the examiner that he should seek out unreported income.

Don't get greedy and try to skim off too much. Start slowly and build it up. At some point, you may be called in for an audit. This is your early warning, which tells you that your declared expenses are arousing suspicion.

The other main point to keep in mind is to watch your lifestyle, and don't flaunt your wealth.

18

LEVEL II: Extra hours, extra work.

This is moonlighting without a visible income. Many people hold part-time jobs, collect paychecks, and suffer through withholdings. Moonlighting for cash, or other untraceable income, is a safe step forward into the underground. Other untraceable income can come from bartering your skills and accepting payment in hard goods or in reciprocal services, as many do. For example, one engineer, who was also a skilled cabinet maker, traded some handmade furniture to the midwife who delivered his wife's baby.

LEVEL III: Operating a business without declaring the income.

Normally, the business must be a sideline, as trying to live without a visible means of support can lead to problems, both with the IRS and with nosy neighbors. A mail-order business is one type of enterprise which is easy to disguise, or even totally bury, because of the nature of the business.

LEVEL IV: Living underground.

This is the radical step of establishing a nomadic existence, suitable mainly for those who so much detest paying taxes that they're willing to adopt a totally different lifestyle in order to avoid paying them. It means taking a job under a false identity, falsifying the withholding form with a claim of extra dependents and a spurious Social Security number, and moving on before any detailed investigation occurs.

This is very difficult to do, and requires a special type of personality. It's *possible* to earn a lot of money this way, and to salt it away in Swiss accounts, but it's not very likely. In practice, almost the only legitimate jobs open to people who can't tolerate a background check are menial ones, those with "no questions asked" and low pay.

Career criminals of various types often live nomadic lifestyles, but they're outside the scope of this book.

HOW TO USE THIS BOOK

This book contains a survey of different ways of earning money as a Guerrilla Capitalist. Not every way is for you. You'll have to assess your skills and preferences realistically to find what's best for you.

It's vital to avoid the mind-set that tells you that you can do anything you want to do. Few of us are so gifted that we can succeed at everything we try. In most fields, few people make it to the top. Anyone who tells you that you can succeed at anything simply by following his plan is merely blowing smoke at you. There's no substitute for hard-core realism.

The best way is to build on what you've got. For example, if you've got a good language skill, and can write clearly and concisely, you might start a resume-writing service. If your skills are mainly manual, if you can fix almost anything even though you have a hard time explaining just how you do it, you might consider appliance repair. Whatever skill you may have, the simplest thing is to use what you've got by applying it to earning money in the underground.

Of course, if you want to do something for which you think you have the talent but are not quite prepared, you may have to invest in education to improve your skill.

The hardest and riskiest way is to branch out into something with which you're totally unfamiliar, however attractive it might seem. You don't know if you'll be able to do it, you'll have to spend money to get training, and you run the risk of crashing, or finding that your effort was a waste because you don't like it after all, or you can't earn enough at it to justify the money you laid out to learn.

This tells you to beware of many promises by various training schools that you can earn BIG MONEY in electronics, or air conditioning repair, or whatever, if you pay them to train you. Unless you're already somewhat acquainted with the field, you have no way of knowing what you'll earn, or whether you'll be able to find work, or even if you have the native ability.

20

All in all, it's best to start out with something that involves the least investment. In many instances, you can get off to a flying start by using what you've already got, without having to sink more money into a fledgling business. For example, if you own your own home, and have an assortment of tools because you do your own repairs, you have a head start at setting up a repair business, which, incidentally, is often a cash business.

In the following pages, we'll survey some good fields as well as some bad ones. The purpose is not only to give you a guide to what you might do, but to warn you of the disadvantages and dangers you might encounter in some areas. There are many of these, and unless forewarned you could find yourself in a sticky situation.

Look over the possibilities carefully, and then decide how *you* want to start. It may be easier than you think.

NOTES

1. *Government By Emergency,* Dr. Gary North, Fort Worth, TX, American Bureau of Economic Research, 1983, pp. 1-49. This gives a clear and convincing explanation, for anyone who hasn't been following the news, of why the Social Security system is in deep trouble, and getting in deeper. It's frightening enough for those old enough to be retiring soon, but the uncertainties of the distant future are particularly serious for those who won't be retiring before the year 2000.

2. *Ibid.*, the rest of the book. Dr. North, along with many other survivalist authors, explains that not only is the Social Security system in trouble, but the whole economy is a house of cards. His view contradicts the consensus of the acknowledged experts in economics, but the experts have been wrong enough times, and about enough questions, to suggest that they are not infallible. On page 41, he describes a book published after the onset of the "Great Depression,"

which quoted many "experts" who said, all through the 1920s, that it couldn't happen.

6

Caveat Entrepreneur

If you're reading this book, and of course you are, then the chances are that you've read others on how to make money. Some of them are realistic, while others are simply mad fantasies. Some promise immense profits to the person who buys and reads the book. A few go so far as to promise that the reader will immediately become fabulously rich without doing any work. The advertisements don't discuss the chances of success and failure. They don't tell you that certain special conditions make their advice impractical for most people.

It's easy to write a come-on. Imagine an ad which says: "SURE-FIRE WAY TO INSTANT MILLIONS." It can be perfectly truthful, but of no help to anyone, because the response, when a sucker sends in his money, is: "Be born rich." That's true, but as practical advice it's about as useful as a condom with airholes for ventilation.

One question to ask yourself, when you see a book advertised promising you instant wealth in a fool-proof way, is: "If this method's so good, what's this guy doing writing a book about it?" In other words: "Why is he wasting his time at the relatively unremunerative craft of writing when he could be out making millions with his sure-fire method?"

Another question: "How many other people have read this book?" Do you really think he's offering the method to

23

you and you alone? What will be the effect of hundreds or even thousands of competitors in the field? Will there be anything left for you?

There are other, more subtle traps. An example is the hypothetical estimate of the money you can earn at a certain pursuit.[1] It's easy to write down figures such as: "With a purchase price of $1.00 each, and a selling price of $2.00, selling one thousand units a day will get you a gross profit of $1000!"

That's perfectly true, but it's not based on a real case, or a real volume of sales. How do you know that you'll sell 1000 units per day? What will your advertising costs be?

Another trap is an overly conservative estimate of the amount of work required. Many businesses, especially franchises, are of the type that require the operator to put in twelve to fourteen hours per day, and sometimes more than five days per week. Many people, seeing a business opportunity for the first time, see only the potential profits, and not the problems that require them to put in prodigious amounts of time.

In fact, some seemingly lucrative businesses do provide good incomes, but if you calculate the hourly wage, the picture is quite different. The small entrepreneur often becomes a slave to his business, and wishes that he were back working for a wage because a regular job wouldn't consume so much of his time.

BEWARE OF BROKERS

There's a plethora of books advising readers on "sure-fire" ways to get rich in real estate or the stock market. These books emphasize the positive aspects, some to the point of dishonesty. Some never mention the drawbacks and risks involved in their money-making plans.

The biggest drawback in real estate or stock market schemes is the broker. To buy or sell anything in either field, it's necessary to deal through a broker. The broker doesn't work for free. He gets a commission on every sale. This brings out one of the outstanding and annoying characteristics of brokers — they encourage people to buy and sell, giving them "tips" about hot new properties, and other inducements. Their money is not at risk. They gain from each deal.

Some brokers carry this to an extreme, operating "boiler rooms," filled with telephone sales people, to generate business for them. Anyone considering dealing in real estate or the stock market should keep this in mind before making any deals.

The media, spoon-fed information by stockbrokers, perpetuate the myth that an active market is a sign of economic health. In one sense, it is. An active market, with many people buying and selling, is very healthy for the brokers. The traders, however, all have to pay commissions on whatever they earn. In one sense, commissions are worse than taxes. The IRS only taxes income, and someone who loses money on a deal doesn't have to pay taxes on it. But the broker collects his commission, win or lose, rain or shine. An investor with a stock holding that takes a catastrophic downturn probably will hear his broker advise him to dump it immediately, and cut his losses. Of course! The broker earns himself another commission while the investor takes a bath.

Real estate is as rocky as the stock market. But there are some additional pitfalls. While real estate brokers are open about their fees, which are commissions expressed in percentages, they're not eager to tell a client about the hidden expenses of buying and selling, which the client finds out when closing a deal. In addition to the commission, there are various filing fees, loan generating fees, "points" to pay if a mortgage is involved, a fee for photographing the property, an escrow fee, appraisal fees, title insurance, and many others which vary from state to state. A person who buys or sells a piece of real estate soon finds out that the system is set up so that everyone has a hand in his pocket.

In real estate, it is possible to consummate a deal without working through a broker, but this usually requires a lawyer, who also charges a fee. There may be no saving at all.

A major disadvantage of the broker system is that all transactions are documented. This shuts out many people in the underground economy. While many investors deal in stocks or real estate as tax dodges, exploiting the many loopholes, they can't hide a cent of any income, but must find ways to shelter it to avoid taxes. This massive documentation is a horror to the Guerrilla Capitalist. Most prefer to avoid it.

MORE WARNINGS

If you've ever looked at the ads for make-money-at-home schemes in newspapers and magazines, you might have wondered if one of them might be for you. If you've ever answered one, you know, and you can stop right here and skip ahead.

These are rip-offs. The U.S. Postal Service warns against them, and you can pick up a leaflet about them at your local post office. They're simply mail fraud, no more, no less.[2]

One type of ad is the "address envelopes" ad, which promises you an attractive rate of pay for addressing envelopes. This is very appealing and attracts a lot of suckers. These ads have been running for decades, which means there's some money in this business for the person running the ad. The problem is that the outfit running the ad doesn't actually provide work, but merely a set of instructions on how to address envelopes and perhaps a list of direct-mail companies to contact. Unfortunately, envelope addressing by machine is far cheaper than with human labor, and there's very little market for this service for the person working at home. Another drawback is that companies usually pay by check, which brings a problem to the undergrounder.

Another enticement is the "blind ad" that often appears in the job classified section of the newspaper. This sort of ad doesn't specify the type of work, and often doesn't even list the company. It promises a high rate of pay for anyone who responds, and specifies that no experience is required. It might even specifiy that there's no selling.[3]

The first and most obvious problem with this sort of ad is that if the offering were really as lucrative and easy as it promises, there'd be no need to advertise. They'd have no trouble finding and retaining people. What the ad doesn't say is always as significant as what it does. There's usually a cash investment required, and the business is merely the bottom end of a pyramid selling scheme, in which whoever answers the ad is really the ultimate customer, and buys a large inventory which then sits unsold in his garage.[4]

Another possibility is that such a blind ad is a come-on for an unattractive door-to-door selling scheme. In one instance, an ad for a "Part-time Personnel Manager" was a come-on for a vacuum cleaner sales company.[5]

Such jobs are not really jobs. In every instance, even with the large and reputable direct sales companies such as Fuller Brush, the applicant signs a contract which states that he's an independent dealer, and buys the products at a discount and sells them to the customers. "You eat what you sell" is the principle, as the dealer's income is by direct commission, and dependent on how much he sells. We'll go into this in more detail in the chapter on door-to-door selling.

Summing up, we see that these blind ads are enticements for "jobs" that are so undesirable that nobody would respond if the ad stated the offering outright.

BE REALISTIC

Many small business schemes simply aren't realistic, and neither are the people who promote or follow them. Some promise or expect immediate riches, intoxicated by the prospect of wealth. Others take on clearly impractical or unprofitable lines, inevitably to be disappointed.

27

Attitude is important, but it's vital not to exaggerate the role of attitude. The widely touted "positive attitude" is a scam, pure and simple. This is the technique promoters use to browbeat their victims when the schemes don't work out. They tell them that the failure is due to their bad attitudes. This absolves the promoters from any responsibility for the failure.

The proper attitude is that of hard-core realism, understanding the problems involved, and looking for ways to solve them. Some people don't understand this, feeling that anything less than an enthusiastic, "rah-rah" attitude will lead to failure because they're not thinking positively.

There's a big difference between realism and defeatism. Promoters who advertise money-making schemes don't want you to realize this. They don't want you to look critically at their schemes, preferring that you accept their claims without any doubts or reservations whatever.

You must also take the same realistic and critical attitude towards any money-making ideas you create. Ask yourself, honestly, if it will work. Is there a market for your goods or services? How do you know? Do you know anyone else who has made this work? If so, why did it work for them? Can you do the same? If it failed, why? Can you resurrect the idea and make it work for you, avoiding the mistakes the others made? How much will it cost to get started? Can you afford to lose that much, if you fail? What are the risks?

Only by appraising your chances realistically will you get a good start in a new venture.

THE DANGERS OF STARTING COLD

According to the Small Business Administration, 85% of small businesses fail within five years. There are several reasons for the failures, among them the simple lack of knowledge and ability, failure to assess the market correctly, and undercapitalization.

The most common one is becoming overextended, according to the SBA, either through starting out without enough working capital or spending too much through over-optimism. A business that takes on too many debts and overhead costs will go broke.

Fortunately, the nature of underground businesses enables Guerrilla Capitalists to avoid these dangers. In fact, because of the peculiarities of the underground economy, you can start cold with a greater margin of safety and fewer risks than the overt businessman.

You usually don't have the overhead and additional expenses that a formal businessman has. As you'll most likely operate out of your home, you won't have the overhead of renting a shop or an office. Because you start small, you won't have employees, at least not in the formal sense.

Formal, above-ground employees would compromise your effort to remain invisible to the government. If you have someone working for you, in the regular sense, you have to withhold taxes from his pay, and turn them into the IRS each quarter. This tells them right out that your business exists. You, in effect, become a tax collector for the government, and of course, you want to avoid this.

Lacking skill is an important start-up danger. Some people misjudge their abilities, thinking that a certain task is easier than it is, or that they'll be able to pick it up quickly enough to carry them through. Elsewhere we deal with the question of picking up a skill, and how to do it quickly and cheaply, without investing in formal education.

The problem of a market is critical. It's easy to say that you'll start out in what seems a lucrative business, but finding customers is another problem. You'll need a certain minimal selling skill to find potential customers, convince them that you can provide a product or service that they need, and persuade them that buying from you is the best choice for them.

Sometimes the market simply doesn't exist. There are some products and services that simply don't sell well. In some fields, there is such intense competition from established businesses that the small undergrounder starting up will be choked off at the outset.

The undergrounder faces many of the risks of the small businessman starting up. However, he has a tremendous advantage. Because he usually starts his operation as a sideline, without heavy investment and without depending on it for a living at first, he doesn't have to be an instant success. He can afford failure. It won't kill him.

Let's deal with the prospect of failure. The hard fact is that there is a very good chance of failure. Bearing up under it and recovering is the most important part of failing. As an undergrounder, if you start small, don't expect too much, and don't depend on your new business to make you a million bucks the first few months, you'll be able to learn from your mistakes, and do a better job of it the next time.

NOTES

1. *The Flea Market Handbook,* Robert G. Miner, Mechanicsburg, PA, Main Street Books, 1981, p. 7.

2. *Guerrilla Capitalism*, Adam Cash, Port Townsend, WA, Loompanics Unlimited, 1984, pp. 87-88.

3. *Opportunity Knocks*, Issue #31, 1978, pp. 2-3.

4. *Ibid.*, p. 3.

5. Personal experience of the author.

7

Business Basics

Traditionally, businessmen keep three sets of books. One is for the day-to-day running of the business. One is for the taxman, showing a pessimistic picture of the profits. And one is to show prospective buyers, exaggerating the profits.

Whether an undergrounder will keep books at all is another question. Anyone who operates totally underground, without the IRS even knowing that he's running a business, would be foolish to keep records. Documentation supplies prima facie evidence of a business's operations, and lays the case right in the lap of a government prosecutor.

An example from the world of crime is the prostitute who keeps a "John list," to aid in keeping track of clients. The list contains all relevant information about a customer: name and address, sexual kinks and preferences, whether he pays well and/or leaves a tip, etc. When vice officers raid a call girl, they always look for a John list because this gives evidence to support a prosecution. The list shows that she is running a business, and the size of that business.

The quasi-undergrounder, who has an underground sideline to his regular business, will of course, keep books, showing exactly what he wishes to show, and no more. This is because he has to maintain a front for the IRS and other agencies.

The pseudo-undergrounder, who maintains a home business to provide a peg on which to hang many deductions, has to keep books, and they have to be as complete as possible, because the better his business is documented, the better case he'll have for justifying his deductions. Someone who, for example, takes work home with him to do in his "office," will need a log of time spent, and a careful collection of all receipts to back up his deductions. He will need copies of his mortgage payment checks, utility receipts, and others so that he may assign a proportion of these bills to his "business expenses."

Keeping the books is only one part of running a business, and there are many "management" theories and practices, but college courses in business administration are so insubstantial as to be all but worthless.

Butch, a successful small businessman, had this to say about the technique of running a business: "It's mostly common sense, and avoiding the mistakes some people make. That's it, really, avoiding the big and expensive mistakes. I've seen guys with degrees, but no common sense, make some bloopers that a kid wouldn't make. They get overconfident, and then careless, and they make a mistake that sinks them."

Butch does acknowledge, however, there is some nuts-and-bolts knowledge essential to running a business, and that this depends a lot on the nature of the business. Most of it comes through practical experience — "on the job training."

The technical end is usually specialized, and each businessman must learn it for himself. Other aspects are somewhat more generalized, such as the field called "personnel." This is merely hiring and directing employees, and most of it depends on the businessman's personality. Some people have an intuitive knack for this; others don't, no matter how many courses in interpersonal relationships they have under their belts.

The nuts-and-bolts aspects of bookkeeping aren't very complicated for the small businessman, and there's no point in rehashing them here when there are many books available on the subject.[1] A superficial knowledge of business law, especially as it applies to taxes, definitely helps, and the rest is already part of most people's experience. Almost everyone knows what a "lien" is, and few don't know what the term "purchase order" means. A college degree in business administration just isn't necessary to run a small business, and most small business owners don't have one.

Learning the basics is usually part of working for someone else, which is where most of us start. Making the most of the opportunity to learn at someone else's expense, and then filling in the gaps with brief study, helps to prepare for independence.

COMMON BUSINESS PROBLEMS

Underground or not, businessmen face similar problems, and can solve some of them in similar ways.

Collection. This is an extremely wide-spread problem, and it's important to note one recurring theme: businessmen often try to work with other people's money. The longer they can delay payment, the longer they can keep the funds earning interest for them.

They have a set of priorities, based on need. It all depends on who needs whom more. Thus, the telephone bill always gets paid on time. The telephone company won't stand for any nonsense from deadbeats, and their means of retaliation is quick and effective — cutting off service.

The beginning businessman is insecure, and often hesitates to do or say anything that might offend a client, such as asking for payment. After a few knocks, his attitude hardens, and he starts to expect payment within a reasonable time.

One bad aspect of letting a client run up a bill too far is that past a certain point, he's got you. The customer who owes you a lot of money has the power to hurt you. Your

33

business may fold if he fails or refuses to pay. While it's always possible to seek a solution in court, this takes time, and the intentional deadbeat is skilled at spinning out lawsuits for months, finding one excuse or another not to appear, asking for an adjournment, and using other delaying tactics. Meanwhile, his creditor suffers, as he needs money to operate his business and pay his bills.

Some operators use this as leverage, forcing small businesses to carry them for fear of non-payment. They'll dole out checks at a slow and measured pace, always staying 90 or 180 days behind, and keep the small businessman on the hook for years, if he lets them.

The remedy is to insist on prompt payment. Getting the leverage to do so is simple. First, diversify your business and have as large a clientele as possible. That way, no major client can sink you. For this and other reasons, many small accounts are better than one or two large ones.

With many clients, dumping a deadbeat doesn't hurt as much, so making the decision to do so is much easier.

Gaining Customers. This is vital. Without clients, a business can't survive.

One intangible factor that's important in building up a clientele is reputation. It's important to build up a good one, by being honest and reliable. Meeting your commitments will do a lot in this regard. No client is unimportant. He can pass the word and bring you another customer.

Having a number of small accounts helps your sense of security. Inevitably, clients go sour. They move away. They die. They no longer need your services. This is why you have to keep seeking new customers.

However, you can over-reach yourself in doing so, getting so many customers that you can no longer service them all. This is why it's important to develop a sense of rhythm for your business.

When business is slow, prospect for new clients. When it's busy, service the ones you've got, and don't worry about getting new business that you can't handle.

34

Keeping Customers. Your reputation, based on the quality of service you provide, is the main ingredient in retaining clients. Unless you're in a one-shot business, and follow a policy of hit-and-run, you need repeat business, and you won't get it unless you keep most of your customers happy. This means ironing out problems before they arise, and being up-front with your clients.

If, for example, you have trouble meeting a schedule because of lack of supplies, or a heavy workload, it's better to tell your customer as soon as you become aware of the problem. Kidding him along, and then letting him down, will arouse resentment. He may well accept the "job," and pay you for it, but won't come back to you if he thinks that you've been dishonest with him. You may offer the lowest price, but if he holds a personal grudge against you, he'll close you out.

Picky Customers. While it's true that you can't please everybody, that doesn't mean that you shouldn't try to please most of your clientele. That's the basis of your business. Nevertheless, you'll find that some customers are very hard to please, and that nothing you can do will keep them happy.

Some customers are nit-pickers. They find fault with everything, and ask you to do the work over, perhaps several times. Advertising agency people are notorious for this. One typesetter, who dropped his ad agency accounts, said that they "pick fly-shit out of the pepper."

Sooner or later, with such problem accounts, you'll have to decide whether you're making or losing money on them. When an unreasonably picky customer bounces your work, you have to do it over, but usually can't collect any more money for it. This can lead to your spending more time on an account than it's worth.

If you're busy, you have to realize that the time you spend servicing such an account takes away from more profitable ones. At that point, you should complete your last commitment to him and leave, not asking for any more business. If he asks you to do another job for him, decline politely.

Dropping Accounts. Dropping an account sometimes requires finesse. The old saying, "Walk out, but don't slam the door," is applicable here. If you do anything to antagonize your account, he'll be vindictive and spiteful. You can be sure that he'll tailor the truth to suit him in telling the story to others. A slow payer, for example, will tell others that the quality of your work was unsatisfactory, never mentioning that he kept you on the hook for an unreasonably long time.

These people can hurt you. That's why it's necessary to "massage" them when you cut them off. Tell them that you'd like to continue, but...

The best way to get rid of a troublesome account is to give him very long delivery dates. If he needs his work in a week, tell him, "Gee, I'd like to do this job for you, but I'm already committed to some others and I won't be able to get to it for a couple of months."

Stealing. People can, and will, steal from you. Some may try to steal tangible items, such as products and supplies. Others will steal ideas. Commercial artists steal from each other constantly.

There's some protection against physical theft. It's possible to prosecute. Protection against theft of ideas is much more difficult.

Some artists will "adapt" a design, changing a few details in order not to make it too obvious. Writers plagiarize often, calling it "research." By paraphrasing, they can give the illusion of original work.

There's no fully satisfactory solution to this. Each protective measure brings new and more ingenious methods of theft.

Bribes. Bribes start with small things, such as giving a customer a present at Christmas. Some customers start to expect such gratuities. Others demand them. Above ground, this is widespread. Fortunately, it isn't common in the underground economy.

A good rule for the small businessman to follow is not to give gratuities of any sort. However, this is almost impossible to practice. It's often necessary to invite a customer out to lunch, which is one way it starts. Keeping it down to a dull roar is the best that most of us can manage.

Normal business problems will always be with us. Coping with them requires some ingenuity, and a little mental toughness. Otherwise, we can lose everything we've built up.

NOTES

1. *Homemade Money,* Barbara Brabec, White Hall, VA, Betterway Publications, Inc., 1984, gives a fairly complete once-over of business terms and practices. Its "A to Z Business Basics," beginning on page 63, gives and alphabetical listing of the rudiments of such subjects as accounting, bad checks, business loans, contracts, the Federal Trade Commission, insurance, labor laws, licenses, patents, recordkeeping, sales tax, telephone, and many more.

8

Avoiding the Credit Trap

Ronald earned a living wage as a city employee. He also moonlighted at various jobs at various times, working weekends at pest exterminating and other pursuits, all of which he arranged through his many friends who took steps to keep him "off the books." His yearly income was substantial, but although unmarried, he was always caught short, always in debt, and always seemed to need more money.

The reason for his chronic financial bind was simple: he was addicted to buying on credit. His wallet was filled with plastic, not paper. We already know the value of paper money is shaky. Inflation beats up the value of your cash supply, and each year brings with it a reduction in your purchasing power. Plastic is far worse.

With credit cards, and revolving charge accounts, you pay dearly for the privilege of spending your money. It's surprising how many people complain about the copious way the government spends money it doesn't have — and yet in their personal lives adhere to the same practices.

Ronald is a good example. Let's look at only one card in his wallet, a bank credit card. He used the revolving feature to the limit. He charged purchases to the end of his line of credit, which for this card was one thousand dollars. Each month, he paid in enough to reduce his balance so that he could buy more, bringing it up to the limit again. He didn't realize that, in effect, he was paying interest on one thousand dollars all year long, reducing his buying power by that amount.

This is serious. Let's see how the figures add up.

Bank card interest rates are high, usually between eighteen and twenty percent, as of this writing. By the time this book reaches print, they may have gone higher. Twenty percent of one thousand dollars is two hundred dollars. Ronald had two hundred dollars amputated from his spending power with this one bank card alone!

> *A further look at figures:*
> 100% income
> -24% income taxes (rough figure)
> -6% sales taxes (again, rough figure)
>
> 70% left for you.
> -20% credit charges
>
> 50% net spendable income.

We see that, in this simplified example, credit charges are only four percent lower than the income tax rate. Of course, there is more to it than that.

First, the twenty-four percent tax figure is an approximation. You might be in a higher or lower bracket. To find out what you're really paying in taxes, look at the bottom line on your tax return, after exemptions and deductions, and see what the government is really assessing you. Next, does your state have an income tax? Most of them do. Calculate that into your figures. Does your city have an income tax? Count that, too.

There are other taxes to figure in, for certain purchases. Is what you're buying imported? Then there are customs "duties," another name for taxes. Are there excise taxes on what you're buying? If so, count those in, too.

Are you buying an airline ticket? Believe it or not, there's a tax on that, too, above the regular sales tax. However, it won't appear on your ticket, as it's supposed to be a secret.

Regarding sales taxes, most localities do not charge sales tax on food bought over the counter, as in a supermarket, although restaurant bills are subject to sales taxes. Check this out next time you're at the market. Maybe you live in a jurisdiction that does tax food.

Now we get to credit. The figure above assumes that all of Ronald's purchases are on credit. Almost nobody buys everything on credit, so to that extent it's unrealistic. However, many people buy their large dollar items on credit, and this adds up quickly.

It's practical to carry a credit card or two, for emergencies. You might need a tankful of gasoline, and not have much cash on you. You might have a tire blow out, or have to stay overnight at a motel because the road home is flooded out. You might also see something that's such a good buy you can't pass it up. All of these are sensible purposes for using credit cards.

On the other hand, if you've made credit buying your lifestyle, you're voluntarily submitting to private taxation that reduces your buying power both in the short run and long run. The worst credit situation (for you, not the bank or finance company) is the revolving account that's stretched to the limit.

One credit card account, with a limit of one thousand dollars, can only let you subject yourself to confiscation of two hundred dollars of your hard-earned money each year, roughly. The problem is that many people don't stop there. They have more than one card.

Credit cards are easy to get. In fact, until a few years ago, when a new Federal law put a stop to it, credit companies used to send credit cards to people who had not even applied for them, in the expectation that once the cards were in their wallets, they'd use them. Even today, getting a new credit card is not hard. All that's necessary is to fill out an application. If you already have a credit card, and have been making payments, you're "home free," which is a bad expression because it's not "free" at all.

Tommy was an impulse buyer. Each week, he'd see something advertised and decide he "needed" it, and would put it on his card. Another problem was that his wife was that way, too. Both of them worked, Tommy for a newspaper and she for the telephone company, and their combined incomes were more than adequate. They had no children, and should have been able to get along very well on their earnings, despite the Federal income tax. Actually, they were almost always "strapped." Because of the incessant hemorrhage in their financial situation, Tommy drove a beat-up old car that he felt he should have scrapped long ago, but couldn't afford to buy a new one. They lived in a ramshackle house in a declining neighborhood, because the mortgage payment was low and they felt that they couldn't afford to move to a more expensive house.

Tommy and his wife are typical Americans. They are trapped by the "system," *but only because they let themselves be enslaved.*

Are *you* this way? Be honest. You don't have to tell me. You're reading what I'm writing, but I can't know what you're thinking.

Do you think you'd like to break out of this trap, if you're in it? Do you want to badly enough to take a couple of unpleasant steps to do so? If not, skip to the next chapter.

If you want to reduce your credit dependency, start by cutting down on your credit purchases. Make it a rule, one you won't break, that you won't buy anything more on credit unless you know that you can pay off the entire balance this month, when the bill comes.

There will be occasional emergencies. That's all right. Put the absolutely necessary purchase on your card, but reduce the rest of your spending to make up for it.

The result will be that you won't, if you're stretched to the limit, be putting anything on your plastic account until it's all paid off. You really shouldn't need to. If you've been spending to the limit, you probably have many of the goodies that money can buy, anyway, such as a couple of color TVs, a stereo, a videotape machine, a few guns, perhaps a pool table, etc. You can entertain yourself with these while you're passing up those glittering new toys you see advertised.

There's a fancy name for what I'm advising you to do, one that the professors in business administration schools love to use, because it's arcane jargon: "Zero-Base Budgeting." What this means in plain language is: *Don't spend anything, anything at all, unless you can justify it anew.*

Ask yourself, before you lay out a dime: "Is this purchase really necessary?" You might find that it's not.

Consider every expense. Do you buy your lunch each day? Why? Because you've always done it? Do you have to keep doing it? Would you consider "brown-bagging" until you get your finances in better shape?

How much gas do you buy for your car? Is each trip necessary? Would better planning save you some mileage? Are you able to combine several shopping trips into one? Do you drive to a shopping center on a Saturday afternoon to window-shop, to kill time? Don't do it. Stay home and entertain yourself there.

Of course, you have to buy food. You might be able to save a little on that, as long as you don't go overboard and attempt the impossible. Don't suddenly go on a saving binge and buy only hamburger if you're used to eating steaks and chops. You might, however, be able to cut down on the number of times a week you eat Porterhouse. If you eat out a lot, that's a definite area to save money. A dinner out costs far more than it costs to prepare at home. In fact, you can often have steak at home for what it costs to eat a hamburger and fries out.

42

Cutting down on your eating is a psychological strain. Cutting down on waste can be satisfying. Are you one of those people who leaves a lot on his plate, or who prepares big portions and has a lot of left-overs? Some people who generate left-overs don't like to eat them. They leave them in the refrigerator until they throw them out. In that case, it's economical to prepare smaller amounts, and cut the waste.

What it all boils down to is: Can you reduce an extravagant lifestyle to get more real value from the money you spend? If you can, you'll secure an advantage for yourself.

Now we come to the payoff. What have you sacrificed for, anyway? Let's look at some figures again.

You're avoiding spending 20% of your money after taxes for interest. What will you now do with it?

Put it in the bank. While it's true that often the rate of inflation absorbs the interest you get from a savings account, it's still not as bad as paying twenty percent to the finance company. You now get eight percent interest on the money you would have paid out.

The payoff is that, if you now want a high-dollar item, you can take the money out of your savings account and pay cash, avoiding the interest charges, and thereby have more disposable income. You'll be able to buy one-fifth more, if you spend all of it, and if you can save some of it, in the long run it'll earn you some interest, enabling you to buy more.

"Wait a minute, now," you say, "What's this about a bank account, if bank accounts leave a paper trail that the IRS can follow to trace your income?"

Let's consider that question carefully. A bank account can be very useful if you're not in the underground economy, but earning a wage from a regular job. Even if you are working a side-line, if what you put in the bank is a reasonable figure, it won't attract attention. You'll have to pay tax on the interest you earn, but that won't be very much.

What if you just don't like banks, or if you don't want to pay the IRS a cent more than you absolutely have to? There are a couple of answers to this.

1. Put the money in a cache in your back yard. It won't earn any interest, but it will form a core of untraceable savings.

2. Buy silver (pre-1964) coins, still legal tender, but not liable to destruction by inflation like paper money. This can be very important if you're a survivalist. Silver coins are definitely good investments if you're economically-oriented and are concerned with the effects of inflation.

3. Invest your liberated money in something that will help you earn more in the underground economy. If you're a plumber, for example, you might want an extra set of tools to take with you when you moonlight. Pay cash, of course.

Arranging your personal finances to make the most of your income is just good sense. We have good reason to berate the government for spending money it doesn't have, thereby creating inflation and increasing the national debt.

But what we *can* control is what we do ourselves. The government can only tax us; it can't force us to spend what we have left after taxes. That's up to us. That's where we make it or break it.

9

Make Full Use of
Your Regular Job

Unfortunately, people see their full-time jobs merely as means of earning money, and ignore the unofficial "fringe benefits" they can acquire. Others, with a little more understanding, see their jobs as steppingstones to better ones, and try to learn as much as they can to prepare themselves for higher-paying jobs.

There are many ways in which you can exploit your job for your own benefit, and learning as much as you can is only one of them. Let's look at the various ways in which you can take advantage of what your employer has to offer.

KNOWLEDGE

Whether the company has a formal training program or not, there's usually the opportunity to upgrade skills, either by on the job training or by gaining additional experience. The supreme fact about knowledge is that you take it with you when you go. You can't walk off with the boss's tools, or computer, or supplies, but the knowledge in your head is invaluable because he can't prevent you from taking it with you.

Most employers are very interested in a job applicant's recent experience, and in many specialized fields there are no training schools to impart the knowledge and skills. On the job training is the only way to get it, and this makes almost any job in that field a steppingstone to a better-paying one.

The one limitation is certain fields which involve "trade secrets." In some areas, especially those involving advanced technology, the applicant has to sign an agreement that he will not reveal any proprietary information, the legal term for "trade secrets." Most employment doesn't fall into this category.

The ultimate is, of course, using what you've learned to start your own business, either full-time or as a form of moonlighting.

CONTACTS

In most fields, it's almost impossible to avoid making contacts, meeting other people in the same line of work. These can be valuable sources of information. Often, the "hidden job market" operates exactly this way. An acquaintance working for another company may tell you of an opening, which enables you to apply for the job before it goes on the open market.

There's other valuable information available through contacts. Job advertisements rarely mention pay, but word-of-mouth can reveal to you what the pay is. Trade contacts pass on information about conditions in the field. For example, you may learn that a certain company pays very poorly in comparison with others in the same area. If the boss is a problem personality, you'll never find out about it from a newspaper ad, or at an employment agency. A friend who works at a company that interests you can pass on much informal "inside" information that will help you make a better decision.

Contacts can be very helpful, which makes a closer look at them worthwhile.

People often associate informally with other people with whom they work. The proportion varies with the trade or profession. Policemen and doctors have almost incestuous social practices, rarely mixing with those outside their fields. Those in other lines, however, are fairly loose, picking their friends according to personal compatibility rather than occupational category. Nevertheless, many people associate socially with fellow employees. Sometimes, when friendships ripen, these associations continue even when the employee leaves the company. If you know someone who used to work with you and now works for another company, he can be your pipeline into that company. You also are surely working with someone who came from another company, and he can provide you with much unofficial information.

Trade shows and conventions offer wide opportunities for information-gathering. You meet people from many other companies, and it's relatively easy to strike up an acquaintance. It's often not necessary to "pump" for information, as many people talk freely about their work. In fact, some people complain about the amount of "shop talk" they hear.

If your work takes you outside your company, if you work as a salesman or truck driver, for example, you meet outside people every day, and these people often serve as sources of information. Even if you don't leave your work-place physically, you many have the opportunity to speak with people on the phone.

Some of the information worth seeking is:

Job openings. What's available? When?

Pay rates. What about fringe benefits? How often are raises? This is very valuable, as some companies offer attractive starting wages, then don't award pay increases, or award them infrequently.

Working conditions. What are the hours? Is there much "pressure" on the job? What's the boss's personality like? Is there much job satisfaction? This last point is particularly important, as many Americans rate job satisfaction highly.

In your case, possibly the most important information you'll find is that relating to part-time work. You might hear of a company which needs a part-time employee. You can find out, directly or indirectly, if the employer is willing to pay you "off the books."

One very important fact about part-time work "off the books" is that many employers who agree to this are willing to pay more for the same work because:

(1) They don't have to do the paperwork.

(2) They don't have to pay matching Social Security payments.

(3) They don't have to pay unemployment premiums on off-the-books employees.

(4) Part-time workers are not eligible for fringe benefits that regular employees get.

All of these savings make it attractive for an employer to pay a premium price for part-time labor. An additional consideration is that the part-time work is expendable, which means that if business slows down, the employer will lay him off without qualms of conscience because the part-timer has a regular job.

Not every employer is willing to pay "off-the-books." Some absolutely refuse, while others will if they want the employee badly enough.[1]

You can also find out about opportunities to apply your skills directly, on a contract basis. A good example is Charlie, who worked for a lawn-care service. In his rounds, he discovered by word-of-mouth from the accounts he serviced that there were others who needed lawn care outside of his employer's normal operating area. With full knowledge and permission of his employer, he began servicing these accounts on this own, very conveniently, as he lived on that side of town. After two years, he had enough accounts to provide him with full-time employment, and he left his job and struck out on his own.

USE IT AS AN ECONOMIC BASE

New businesses often have cash-flow problems. At the outset, with few accounts, they often don't provide enough income. At first, you may even have to subsidize your enterprise with earnings from your full-time job. Using your steady job to put the bread on the table while you build up your new business offers you an incomparable advantage. Not only do you have more security, but you can afford to charge lower prices, attracting more customers, than you could if it were your sole source of income.

SEEKING DISCOUNTS

Often, your employer will buy his supplies from regular vendors. These vendors usually are willing to give discounts on tools to employees of their accounts, for the intangible benefit of "good will." This means that they know that the employee may be a boss or supervisor someday, himself ordering supplies, and they want him to have a good image of themselves. You can take advantage of this by buying your own set of tools for your new business.

This relationship can work both ways. While the vendor is procuring your good will, you can be building him up as a regular supplier for the materials you need for your sideline. Not only will this enable you to get supplies later at the usual trade discount, but you'll be able to use him as a dumping ground for third-party checks. In some enterprises, it's impossible to avoid taking checks. These form a dangerous paperwork trail, and you need a way of "laundering" your income. Using these checks to pay for tools and supplies is one excellent way of doing it, as they will never appear in your bank account.

ETHICS

This oft-neglected topic is worth a close look, as people like to feel good about what they're doing, to feel they are moral persons. There is a lot of counterfeit morality, though, which often misleads people into seeking less for themselves than they might if they had more realistic views of the real world of business.

An excellent example is company loyalty. An employer will often expect his workers to be loyal to an unrealistic degree, while offering nothing in return. He expects two weeks' notice when an employee quits, but lays off or fires people with no notice at all.

Also concerned with company loyalty is the problem of "conflict of interest." An employer expects that his employees will not work in competition with him. One who runs a plumbing shop, for example, may demand that his employees not moonlight, either for themselves or another company, in competition with him, although he employs several people and tacitly sets them up in competition with each other.

This is a subtle point, and many employees don't realize that they're being set up in competition with each other. When business slows down, for example, the employer will tend to lay off the least productive worker. When awarding pay increases, they usually go to the employees whom he considers most valuable. The employer who awards promotions on the basis of ability forces his employees to compete among themselves for the slot.

The employee who leaves and starts dealing with his former boss's customer, in direct competition with him, will arouse the anger of the employer. He'll accuse him of "stealing," or "pirating" his accounts. Yet, many businessmen take over the accounts of others, and may even have started in business by "pirating" the account of someone for whom they once worked.

Jack B. was a salesman for an employer whom most people described as "paranoid," or "unstable." Irving G., the employer, had a violent temper and brooding personality, and even his most loyal employees didn't stay for more than three years. Jack B. decided to start his own company, in direct competition with Irving, and was extraordinarily successful. Not only did he take with him most of the best accounts, but also Irving's most productive workers. Within a year, Irving had filed for bankruptcy.

Usually, the employee who pockets company property knows that this is theft, and that it's wrong, by custom, religious doctrine, and by law. The picture is not as clear when dealing with the intangibles, and an employee may often be misled into observing a code of fairness and morality that's very one-sided.

Some employers expect their workers to put in extra hours without compensation. This is, bluntly, stealing the employee's time. While the payment of overtime is usually regulated by state labor laws, the worker who is victimized by this finds it hard to bring a grievance because he faces the day-to-day problem of putting bread on the table, and is afraid of losing his job. A court victory in several years' time will not feed his family tomorrow.

What you do is up to you. You'll make your decision according to your personal code, and according to how fairly you feel your employer is treating you. A lack of fairness is why many employees steal, feeling that they're simply ripping off the boss in compensation for his ripping them off.

A lot depends, therefore, on what you think of the way your boss treats you. If he's a "stand-up guy," you'll probably be reluctant to do anything questionable. If you see him as unfair, unethical, or sneaky, you'll probably feel that you have the license to compromise with your normal ethics, the only restraint being to avoid getting caught.

More depends on you than on him. People vary a lot in how they see themselves and others. You might feel, if you have a very unfair, unethical employer, that anything goes. You might, on the other hand, feel that you won't put yourself down at his level, and simply find another job.

NOTES

1. *Guerrilla Capitalism,* Adam Cash, Port Townsend, WA, Loompanics Unlimited, 1984, p. 35.

10

Making the Time

Often, a major barrier to setting up an underground business is finding the time. As many of us have our schedules arranged for us, we find little free time and what we do find, we need for relaxation. We're tied up working, commuting, shopping, taking the kids to school, attending Little League games, and many other time-consuming activities.

Mike was a machinist with a problem. He'd been in the field for twenty years, ever since he'd gotten out of the Navy, and was a well-paid journeyman. He'd originally taken a job only a mile from home, but when he got married, his wife insisted they move to a "better" neighborhood. Their new apartment was five miles away from work, still not too far to drive. When their first child was born, his wife made it clear to him that the city's schools were not the best, and they'd be better off moving outside the city.

Mike had a few years to consider this, and on many weekends he and his wife would make trips into the suburbs to look for suitable housing. They looked, picked, and chose, and by the time they'd decided, prices near the city were so high that the only houses they could afford were fifty miles out on the expressway. This was still not too bad, and Mike resigned himself to commuting, as he felt the kids' benefit came first. By this time, they had three, and Mike was very concerned that they grow up in a healthy neighborhood.

As the years went by, Mike's living expenses went up to overtake his income, and commuting got a lot tougher. The entire area was full of developments. Many of the new residents worked in the city, funneling onto the expressway each morning, and by now the trip was taking Mike over two hours each way.

He also could not drive straight to work anymore. Parking around the shop had become impossible, and there was no parking lot nearby. Mike had to drive in to a parking lot just inside the city line, then take a subway train to a place near his job, where he changed to a bus for the rest of the trip in.

When Mike's brother-in-law, who lived in the next town over, started a machine shop in his huge garage and asked Mike if he'd work for him off the books, Mike had to refuse. He simply didn't have the time. Driving home, he thought it over, and realized that between his parking, bus, and subway expenses, he was losing badly by holding onto his present job. He didn't get paid for the time he spent commuting, and the cost of driving, with the sharply increased price of gasoline, had become almost prohibitive. He realized, too, that he had to travel at a much lower speed on the road because of the bumper-to-bumper traffic, and this increased his gas consumption.

Arriving home, he figured it out:

75¢ each for bus and subway, four per day $3.00
Gasoline $5.00
Time, at 10/Hour $40.00
Total $48.00/day

He earned $10.00 per hour, which meant that a normal eight-hour day paid him $80. This totalled out to $400 per week, but his commuting costs ate up a large part of it, $240.

Taking that from his take-home, about $320 after the deductions, left him with $80.00.

"There must be a better way," he thought. He remembered that he'd seen a job opening in the next town, one that paid only $9 per hour, but he calculated his figures again:

Gross pay $360.00

Net pay $290.00

Commuting costs:

Gasoline $5.00/week

Time, ½ hr. x 5@9.00/hr. =................. $45.00

.... -$50.00

Net $240.00

This also left him about eight hours he didn't have before to work in his brother-in-law's shop at $10 per hour, tax-free, and he'd feel better too, because he wouldn't be as tired.

The next day he interviewed for the job, was accepted, and gave notice. In two weeks, he was at his new job, with commuting a pleasure compared to what it had been, and was able to moonlight in the evenings, which added another $200, tax-free, to the family income.

Let's look at the grand totals, counting just take-home.

The previous job paid him $320.00.

The new one pays $290, but the extra $200 off the books added in yields $490. This is without counting time, fuel, and other commuting costs.

Surprising? A lot of people don't realize they spend a lot of time and money they might not have to if they sought another job, even at lower pay.

Commuting is a way of life for many people. In the big cities, many don't realize how disadvantageous it is because they've seen everyone else doing it. Often, commuting costs make a certain job just not worthwhile, and there's a real advantage to changing, even if the new job pays less.

There are three areas of improvement.

(1) *Savings on commuting costs.* As we've seen, this can be a lot.

(2) *Savings on taxes.* Another job, which pays less and yet permits reducing costs, resulting in a net gain, means less withheld in taxes.

(3) **The freedom to seek another money-making opportunity.**

Time is money, and making the best use of it is worth the effort. It's not necessary to schedule every minute of the day, as some recommend, because this obsessive micro-scheduling results in too much pressure. It's better to avoid the large flagrant wastes.

Another way to save time is to double up on it. A person who enjoys his hobby and finds a way to make it pay is relaxing and earning simultaneously.

Another way to is to double up on trips. Many tasks involved in underground money-making require travel. Doubling up on trips saves both time and car expenses. With limited resources, it helps to be able to stretch time.

Making the best use of time is both an art and a science. It's necessary to be well-organized. The sort of person who has the self-discipline to start and succeed at his own business, and is able to manage his money to cope with the problems, is the sort of person who will show a natural aptitude for managing his time as well.

11

How to Brainstorm

Brainstorming for ideas on how to make money is difficult at first for most people. That's why it's helpful to use some cues, the sort you find in the Yellow Pages. Let's let our fingers do the walking and see what kind of ideas we can come up with.

Acupuncturists. Do you do this for a living? No? Well, that's one idea shot.

Hey, wait! How about another healing skill? Do you know any folk medicine? Do you know any home remedies that you could manufacture and sell, under the table?

Air Conditioning. What does this suggest? Repair? Maybe, if you have the skill. But what about preventive maintenance? Can you persuade a few people that, although you don't have the training to repair an air conditioner or evaporative cooler, you have enough smarts to check it out, recharge it, and to do it at lower cost than the punitive prices that air conditioning people charge?

Animal Carcass Removal. This might be worth a phone call. Not because you want to get into the business, but because these companies use animal by-products. Is there much roadkill in your area? Would it pay to keep a couple of boxes and plastic bags in your trunk just in case? What do they pay? A phone call will get you an answer.

Apartments. Right! You have a room you'd like to rent, huh? Well, see about doing it off the books.

Blood Bank. Here's something you might consider, if you're in very good health, and want to earn a few bucks every now and then. A phone call will tell you what they pay, and you can then decide if it's for you.

Book Dealers — Used. Do you pick up scrap paper? Newspapers? Do you ever find any books in the pile? Maybe these people will buy them from you at more than scrap paper price. Ask.

Building Contractors. Maybe you know one who needs casual labor, such as cleaning up a job site. This might not be the job for you, but for your teenager, if the boss pays cash. Find out.

Carpet Cleaners. These people have big commercial machines, but maybe you could still use the carpet cleaner that your wife got you to buy last year, and which sits in the closet most of the time. Ask your neighbors if they want you to clean their carpets, cut-rate. Another idea is that they might rent the machine from you, if you charge less than the supermarket down the road.

Caterers. You don't run a restaurant, but didn't your neighbor complain to you last week about the high estimates he got when trying to find someone to cater a party? Can you do a good job for less? Will your wife (or husband) help?

Cocktail Lounges. You need a license to open a bar, but how about an after-hours club?

Collection Agencies. Sometimes these can use part-time help. Would they accept your contract labor? Would they want to pay you on commission? Call.

Dentists. Dentists use X-ray machines, too, and X-ray film has silver in it. Is this scrap reclaimable? Does your dentist already sell it? If not, will he give or sell it to you? Where can you sell it? Look in the phone book under SCRAP METAL.

Editorial Services. Some small publishers can use part-time proofreaders. This is work you can do at home, and it offers two prospects.

If your client's willing to pay you cash, you can hide the income completely.

If he pays by check, and the volume is large enough that you can't hide it completely, you can still get some benefit, because if you can devote one room of your house or apartment completely to this, you can take an extra deduction. You can also deduct mileage and utilities. It might not be underground, but it's still better than being a wage slave.

Florists — Retail. Do you like gardening? Raising flowers? Next time you're near a florist, take along a few of your flowers as samples. Ask if he'd like to buy from you. You can surely beat the commercial florists' prices, as you do it for a hobby. Ask for cash payment in return for low prices. It's all gravy.

Gift Shops. Do you make macrame or anything else that could serve as a gift? If it's your hobby, you might make it pay. Go to a local gift shop with some samples. Perhaps you can interest the owner in buying from you. For cash, of course.

Hobby Shop. Now here's a live one! Have a talk with the owner. Suggest to him that you might hold classes in one of the hobbies for his customers. It's not likely that he'd be interested in paying you for your instruction, but you might work out a deal, anyway. Suggest that, in return for you holding classes, for which he would not charge the students but which would help stimulate his business, you would be able to buy your hobby supplies from him at cost. This is an example of a trade-out, which is utterly safe because it's untraceable. It happens to be legal, too, because as a businessman, he can charge the prices he wishes.

Janitorial Service. There are many listed in this category, which shows the business is there. One key to determining if there's room for you is if there's much new construction of industrial parks in your area. A new concern is a hot prospect, as you're less likely to find that they have a service and are satisfied with it.

Lawn Maintenance. Ditto. Check new housing developments. Builders often don't even landscape the buyer's lawn anymore. They throw a bag of grass seeds at him and he's on his own. There's potential business among new house buyers.

Maternity Apparel. This offers an unexpected opportunity. If you're a midwife, or a childbirth instructor, don't think you can get referrals from doctors or hospitals. They don't like the competition, and won't give you the time of day from your own watch. A maternity shop is a good place to post a flier advertising your services, however. An excellent approach is to give a freebie to the owner, if she's female and pregnant. Deliver her baby at home and she'll give you a personal recommendation. This can count a lot with her customers.

One possibility is to offer a free orientation course to all customers. This initial session will enable them to see what you have to offer, and you can sign up those who find your service attractive.

Paper Hangers. Can you do this? It's a useful adjunct to painting, and you can get the same sort of customers. This also suggests some ways to advertise; leaving a flier or a short stack of your cards at a wallpaper dealer's. One incentive you can use with the dealer is to offer him a commission on any accounts you get through him, or offer to buy all of your supplies from him.

Reading Improvement Instruction. The only listing here is for Evelyn Wood, a nationwide firm which teaches speedreading. This suggests there's room for you. You don't have to compete with Evelyn Wood. There are many children who have trouble reading. Let's face it, the schools are lousy. If you can read well, and if you are patient and have a good manner with children, you may be able to seek out parents of children who are not reading well and offer your services as a coach or tutor.

Riding Academies. Can you ride a horse? Do you own a horse or two? If so, and if you have the time, you can give riding instruction, cut-rate. Don't try to leave your cards at stables or riding academies, though. Try sporting goods shops, outdoor shops, those specializing in western wear, and saddleries.

Resume Service. The number of listings in this category shows you the business is out there.

Saw Sharpening. Can you do this? If so, you surely have friends and neighbors who'll pay for your service. It won't make you rich, but a few bucks, tax-free... Take it where you find it.

Veterinarians. No, you can't go into competition with them, but if you offer a pet grooming service, you can leave your cards at a vet's. Most likely, you have a pet of your own. Go to your vet and tell him you're in business. To accomodate a customer, he'll let you leave a stack of your business cards on his counter.

Water Softeners. No, not for you, but does it suggest something else, something related to water? Will your neighbors pay you to water their lawns? This is labor-intensive, as they provide the water. Many people forget, or are too involved with other things, to remember to water their lawns regularly. This is a project you can undertake very economically. You don't have to stand by and watch the water flow. When you've got one hose deployed, walk down to your next account and set his up, then to the next, etc. By the time you've made your rounds, it's time to shut off the water at the first one.

THE BIG PICTURE

The U.S. Department of Labor has a huge volume listing all occupations with their code numbers. It has well over thirty thousand between the covers, yet it's almost useless for your purpose. You can find a copy at the local office of the state employment service, and perhaps in your local library but don't waste your time looking.

You can go blind looking at the fine print. It also doesn't list all occupations, because the people who compiled this volume simply don't understand all the sub-specialities in each broad category. In any event, the official names of these occupations are not very useful or thought-stimulating.

The Yellow Pages are best, if you use them properly. One feature of the phone book which you should not overlook is the large number of display ads. The simple listing of names, addresses, and phone numbers doesn't tell you as much as do the ads.

They list what services a company provides, and tell you a bit about the occupation. From this information, you can decide if there's a part of the job you could do. You can also read and infer what they're missing, or overlooking. Maybe there's a gap that you could fill. For example, a construction company produces a lot of scrap on each job. They have to haul it away, and clean up after themselves. Can they use an independent hauler? If you have a pick-up truck, you might offer this service to a small contractor. Don't call the large ones. They have their own trucks and their own full-time hauling services.

Read every display ad carefully for these details. Think about what they offer, and what they don't provide. Don't be discouraged by the size of the phone book, or the huge amount of reading you might have to do. Start with the A's and go from there. The odds are you won't get far down the alphabet before you find something worth following up.

Another value of the Yellow Pages is that the volume gives you specific information. No mere listing of occupations can tell you which companies supply what. No book on side-line jobs or underground money-making, even this one, can tell you what's available in your own neighborhood.

With the Yellow Pages, you can see immediately if anyone is covering a certain field, and make a judgment of how large and successful their operations are by the location and size of their business. This enables you to estimate the competition you'll face.

Scan the phone book, and scan it critically. Keep thinking, and you'll find several hot prospects for earning extra money!

12

Estimating Your Market

Market research is a valuable tool for big businesses, for they have to make decisions concerning millions of dollars' worth of investments, and having a rough guide to the potential returns is a planning tool. Some authorities recommend that the small businessman make his own market survey.

The suggested method is to go out and ask potential customers if they need a product or service of the sort you plan to offer. While this method seems very straightforward and attractive, it has some fatal flaws.

The biggest one is that many people don't do what they say they'll do. Someone who answers hypothetically that, yes, he'd eagerly buy such a product or service may not be willing to shell out the cash when the real moment comes. The promoters of market research don't like to talk about this point, the unpredictability of human behavior.

An excellent example of a market research failure was the Ford Edsel of nearly thirty years ago. Ford, before sinking half a billion dollars into designing and tooling up to produce the Edsel, did market research on the need for such a car. They concluded that the American public, because it had been buying gas-guzzling barges for decades, would willingly snap up more of the same. The rest is history, and Robert

MacNamara, the author of this catastrophic failure, left Ford shortly thereafter to become the Secretary of Defense under the Kennedy Administration, where he applied his methods to the Pentagon.

A better guide than listening to what people say is to observe what they do. This will give you a more accurate idea of whether or not you have something they'll buy. The best guide to people's actions in the future is what they've done in the past, even though conditions change and human behavior changes with them. In this case, the key is that you're changing one of the conditions.

A good example: You're a plumber, seeking some outside work among your friends and acquaintances. From experience, you know household plumbing sometimes fails, and when this happens, people call plumbers. You also know, from experience and observation, that if people have the opportunity to buy the same grade of product or service for less money, they'll most likely do so. As you're already in the business, and have your own tools, you offer your services, and to your gratification, you find that some people will call on you when the toilet or sink backs up, because you charge them less for the same good job they would get from an established plumbing company.

There's always Murphy's Law, and this will foul up the best estimates, introduce a degree of uncertainty into the calculations, and reinforce the need for caution. You'll inevitably find that, of a certain number of potential customers, some simply won't buy when the moment comes. Some die, some move away, and others simply find a better deal elsewhere. The other side of the coin is that you can also pick up new and unexpected customers, which tend to compensate for the ones you lose.

In the end, it boils down to individual judgment, a lot of which is guesswork. This is why it's smart to minimize your initial effort and investment, because that way you minimize your risk.

CALCULATING YOUR SALES AND PROFITS

There are all sorts of accounting methods used to calculate sales and profits. For accuracy, they depend on strict accounting, and this is both their greatest strength and their greatest weakness. As a small businessman, you can't afford the time for meticulous accounting, because that is overhead and doesn't add to your profits. Large companies can tolerate this overhead, partly because they're big, and partly because it's a way of keeping track of information that no single person can hold in his head.

As an underground small businessman, you can, and should, be able to keep track of what you spend and what you're earning, without making extensive notes. A short stack of three-by-five cards is the most you should need, if you want to keep records.

Because you're operating underground, most of the rules that cover business accounting don't apply, anyway. Let's look at the time spent, for example. If you're making money from your hobby, should you count your time as business, or pleasure? You enjoy what you're doing, and would be doing it anyway, so where do you draw the line? The obvious answer is that you count the time that you're spending on a project for money, but even this is not a satisfactory answer. Should you count your other time as overhead, because you're spending it practicing the skill that you sell? The fact is that you'll probably be spending a lot of time on your various projects, and if you stop to count the income per hour you're earning, the answer might be discouraging.

Another example: You're a plumber, and you're doing a job for a friend in his home. Because you're chatting with him while you're working, you're probably working more slowly than if you were working for a stranger. You have a couple of beers while you're working and talking. Do you count the beers as part of your income? After the job is over, you linger and talk awhile, instead of going straight to

66

another job. Do you count this as non-productive time, as part of your overhead?

There are no easy answers, and cost accounting is mostly a waste of time. You'll be better off if you don't bother much with it.

GETTING INFORMATION

This is the first step in setting up an underground business, if you're not already in the field. It can also be very tricky, as there are many traps for the unwise.

Let's look at the worst way of getting information first, answering a business opportunity advertisement. Most of these ads are simply come-ons, promising great wealth to anyone who sends in his money. Most of these ads fall into two types, those which sell equipment and those selling stocks of goods. Equipment is for manufacturing a product, such as rubber stamps, which the ad promises will sell very well with little effort. Stock is a product that also supposedly will sell very well, and is usually part of a "pyramid selling" scheme.

Don't be fooled by these ads, no matter what they promise. In all cases, you are the ultimate consumer, because once you've bought whatever they're selling, you're stuck with it. Be especially wary of the tantalizing ads that tell you nothing about what the product or the scheme is. They're full of teasing lines, to arouse your interest but reveal nothing.

Where, then, do you get reliable information on underground money-makers? The first, and most reliable way, is to have on-the-job experience.

The second choice, ignored by many people, is your local public library. Please note that this information is not free. Your tax dollars are paying for it. Despite this, many people simply don't think of the library as a source of information, although there are sections dealing with all sorts of practical trades. Usually, these are in the 600-numbered section if the library uses the Dewey Decimal System. Ask your librarian for help if you can't find what you need.

A third way is to contact the American Entrepreneur's Association, Suite H-661, 2311 Pontius Avenue, Los Angeles, CA 90064. Phone (800) 421-2300, 2345, 7266, or 7269. These people sell manuals covering many types of businesses, and if you can't find what you need in the local library, try them.

The manuals are expensive, most ranging from about $25 on up, and contain much detailed information. The emphasis is not so much on the technical aspects, but on setting yourself up in business. They cover costs and profits, licenses, location, signs and other advertising, insurance, merchandise and pricing.

These are aimed mainly at above-ground types of businesses, which limits their usefulness to you. You can use these manuals as a basis to determine if the operation you're contemplating is adaptable to the underground.

13

Smaller is Better

It's been a truism in this country, and others, that the future belongs to the large corporations, that there is no room for the small businessman, who will be ruthlessly squeezed out by relentless competition from the conglomerates. Fortunately for those of us who like independence, the picture is not as bleak as this oversimplified version. In reality, the large corporations, although they have the capital for the large investments needed in heavy industry, don't have the flexibility to meet the changing needs of the market. Actually, despite the heavy load of propaganda, the big conglomerates don't hold all the cards.

One reason is simply that people want more than the big companies can provide, and the people who run the large corporations, feeling smug and secure, are not responsive.

An excellent example is the American automobile industry. The executives in Detroit have for years convinced themselves they could, by advertising, dictate the automotive needs of the American people, and compel them to buy their overly large, poorly-made gas-guzzlers. For decades, they had squeezed small manufacturers out of business, until the market became dominated by the "Big Three," or the "Big Four," if we count American Motors.

Since WWII, this has changed, slowly at first, then more quickly. Foreign cars have made a significant advance in the American market, and the people, whom the Detroit executives viewed as mindless sheep responding to their advertisements, have chosen foreign cars in larger numbers, and we've seen the partial collapse of the American automobile industry. Chrysler started slipping down the tubes, and only a massive intervention by the Federal Government prevented a total disaster. The future of the other auto makers is doubtful, as more Americans are discovering that a car can be well-made, and economical to run, and that the best ones come from foreign shores. The energy crisis has made this even more poignant, because large, thirsty cars are simply out of reach for most people who have to live on a budget.

The auto industry is not the only example. The telephone company, with its arrogant attitude and monopolistic pricing, has had serious competition from independents on what traditionally has been its home ground, the manufacture of telephone equipment and long-distance lines. The independent telephone manufacturers, both domestic and foreign, have to stand or fall on the merits of their products, not because they're the only game in town.

There are other examples. RCA Corporation, with its massive and expensive Videocomp, has found little market for it, while Compugraphic, which makes small machines suitable to the decentralized needs of the small businessman, has prospered.[1]

Small printing presses, following the trend, have proliferated, with quick-print shops, both independent and franchised, springing up in every neighborhood. A customer who wants some business cards or some stationery is not going to want to send away to a large, mail-order outfit for them, because this usually means waiting several weeks, and he'd like them sooner. Although the small printer can't provide as low a price as the large company, he can provide better service.

70

Customers run into a couple of other problems with large companies. A mail-order discount printer has shipping costs, which will often eat up any savings in price he can offer. The problem of correcting errors also crops up. A small printer, if there's an error in his work, can quickly run the job again. The customer who orders by mail, on the other hand, often must wait to have the error corrected, and the time is as long as it was for the original order, as the large company, with a backlog of work, makes the customers wait in line.

Returning to the auto industry, we see that, although the manufacturers have set up nationwide organizations for sales and service, small, independent concerns actually do the majority of maintenance and repair work on cars.

An automobile dealership is an excellent example of what can go wrong with growth. A small dealership, in which the owner is both salesman and service manager, is the ideal, even though he may not handle the volume to offer the best prices. Most of us who have bought cars have had the same experiences.

We go into the showroom of "Honest John's," and we run into a friendly, smiling salesman who does everything he can to make us happy and willing to buy a car. He promises the moon, the sun, and the stars, and tells us that his service department is second to none.

Some dealerships even have round-the-clock sales, in which the sales office is open late, twenty-four hours a day. They'll accomodate the schedules of working people in order to sell them cars. Even the most conservative dealers have sales offices that keep longer than usual hours.

When we buy the car, and return for service, it's a different picture. The repair department keeps only normal business hours, and we have to meet their schedules or go without service. We arrive at the service desk, and have to wait in line, instead of getting personal attention of the sort we got in the sales department. The service manager makes it clear, by an attitude that borders on discourtesy, that he'll get to us when *he* feels like it, not at *our* convenience. The message is clear: we've bought the car, and now we're stuck with it.

If we go back to the salesman, expecting him to intervene to help with a special problem, we find that he's washed his hands of the affair once he sold the car. It's not his department now, and he's uninterested in helping.

This is the key to personal service: the person who makes the promises has to be the one to fulfill them. If not, the company is departmentalized, and the salesman can, and often will, promise excellent service knowing he can say what he likes, not being the one who will have to do the work.

In a small company, where the two functions are not separated, we can expect, and often get, better care. We don't have to go through a chain of bureaucracy to meet with the boss. In a large company, the owner is usually unavailable, and isolated from his customers by a gauntlet of receptionists, managers, and unmarked doors.

This is why there's a growing place for the small businessman who takes good care of his customers. While the economics of mass production usually results in a lower price for many manufactured goods, there's more to a business transaction than price alone. People expect more, and they often will favor the small businessman who can provide more.

The large producers are in danger, and many small independents have come on the scene. Part of the reason for this is the distaste people feel at the impersonal service they get from the large companies. Anyone who's had to deal with the telephone company understands this, and resents the frustration of dealing with a low-level employee who speaks like a robot and has no decision-making power. The situation is much the same with other large companies, and the difficulties of getting personalized service, of running into the barriers of "company policy" and working up through the chain of command to settle a simple problem, has had its effect. In dealing with a small company, it's possible to talk with the boss, and to resolve the problem quickly, without a chain of memos traveling up the line and the inevitable delays that this brings.

Americans who work for large corporations get enough of this treatment on the job, and are reluctant to settle for it in their personal lives. This portends well for you, if you're thinking of going into business for yourself. You can provide personalized service, and in fact have little to fear from the large companies, who can't compete with you.

Smaller is better. One serious problem large companies face is that they develop bureaucracies in the same way, and of the same size, as do our various levels of government. This leads to inflexibility. Despite certain economies in large-scale manufacture, there's a point of diminishing returns. Flexibility of response is in many instances as important as price.

We see no conglomerate pizza shops, for example. There are franchises, but the business does not lend itself to mass production in a central plant and nationwide distribution. In any event, mass production is efficient only up to a point, after which the distribution costs outweigh the savings.

This is why many small manufacturing and service companies are emerging. They provide what the big ones cannot. This is true of both the overt economy and its underground counterpart.

The small entrepreneur holds most of the cards in this case. He does not have the high overhead that the large companies sustain. To the extent that he operates underground, he also does not pay the tax burden, and therefore has a competitive edge.

NOTES

1. *The Household Economy*, Scott Burns, Garden City, NY, William Morrow and Company, Inc., 1982, p. 207.

14

More Mileage
From Your Money

Even the least experienced income earner knows that obtaining income is only half the battle. Getting something in return, and making the most use of the few dollars available, is the other half. Unfortunately, most of the attention, both in print and in the other media, is focused on earning, not spending, which leaves the householder in a bind.

There are social and cultural barriers, too. One of the most persistent is "Keeping up with the Joneses," which moves people to spend conspicuously to keep a certain status among their peers. The extreme of this is "All flash and no cash," the spectacle of the high roller without a cent to his name and deeply in debt.

One unfortunate fact about getting an increase in earnings is that spending seems to rise to absorb it. It's bad enough that a raise often leads to "promotion" into a higher tax bracket, something that even Mr. Reagan's "indexing" plan will not help very much (too little and too late), and that inflation seems to absorb the rest, but perversely many people want to have something to show for their enhanced economic status, and buy more.

This is one cultural barrier to getting the most from your money. An economic barrier is credit buying, with which we deal in another chapter. Credit, an unofficial form of taxation, has serious effects. It's true that "a penny saved is *more* than a penny earned."[1] We often see people unwisely taking out unneeded loans, and paying dearly for them.

One enticement that banks and other lenders use is the offer to accept a savings account as collateral for a loan. This means that the borrower earns maybe 8% interest but has to pay as much as 20%, depending on the sort of loan he gets. This is stupid.

Another is buying a house or car on "time" while having the cash to buy it outright. Some people eye the deduction allowed for interest payments, but forget that a deduction is not a refund, that the IRS allows only thirty cents on the dollar for someone in the 30% bracket, and then to get the deduction one has to pay the interest first.

There are limits to what we can save on spending. During the 1960s, many hippies tried to drop out of "the system" and retreated to rural areas to live off the land.[2] While this was practical a century ago, it's just about impossible today. We can take it as an axiom that it's impossible to live without *some* money today. There are two reasons for this.

(1) There is truly no more frontier, no more free and undeveloped land where someone may settle down. All land in this country is either privately owned, or in the hands of the local, state, or Federal government.

(2) The "system" is all-pervasive, and is set up to prevent anyone from "dropping out." Even land is taxed today, and anyone who buys a piece of property must come up with tax money each year. Failure to pay the tax results in confiscation, and the land being sold to pay back taxes. This requires some income, which makes the landowner subject to other taxes as well. The people who run the system fear non-compliance most of all, and they have set it up to make it impossible to live without some sort of participation. Taxation hits both income and spending, and even simple ownership, as with land and motor vehicles. Still, there are

some advantages to the rural life, and some ways to make it work. More about this later.

We can't drop out totally, but we can reduce our dependence on the system drastically, depending on how well we apply ourselves. An example is the person who grows his own vegetables. Growing one's own food can save in several ways, in the costs of labor, profit, distribution, and taxation.[3]

Making spending more efficient isn't penny-pinching. It's getting more from what you spend. The first step is budgeting.[4] This enables you to know what you spent last year, and what you anticipate spending this year. It gives you a handle on the problem. The second step is "Zero-base budgeting," going over each item to see if it's truly justifiable before spending the money. This isn't as hard as it seems, as most of these decisions make themselves. However, there's a need for flexibility and creativity, because often there are unexpected options that enable big cuts in the budget.

In budgeting, you must distinguish between needs and wants. Often, people burden themselves with wants so that they have a hard time taking care of the needs. It's necessary to make a meticulous analysis of needs, and examine ways of obtaining them more cheaply.[5]

Another barrier to enjoying a debt-free lifestyle is cultural. The Protestant work ethic, while is has its positive side, also carries with it some attitudes that are counter-productive and even economically dangerous. The unwritten rule that we must always take a job that pays more than the previous one, gives more status, is "secure" because it's "permanent," and is within our line of work is an intangible but real barrier to living free.[6] This restricts and contradicts a quality that seems to be built into most human personalities, flexibility. This also restricts freedom of choice when there's good economic logic. It makes good sense, for example, to take a lower-paying job if the commuting savings outweigh the cut in pay, but many people can't bring themselves to do it.

There are economic barriers, too, restricting job choices. The larger companies have systems of deferred rewards to keep their employees chained to their jobs. A pension plan is one example. Today, more than ever, a pension plan is a fraud for most employees. He gets nothing until he retires, or at least, becomes "vested." Layoffs and other means of inducing turnover are ways to get rid of employees who are coming close to collecting the promised rewards.

Another cultural barrier is the prejudice against buying second-hand goods. Economic status is important in America, and buying second-hand is a confession of poverty, something which some people fear more than being naked. Actually, many Americans are resigned to buying second-hand cars, but not many to buying second-hand clothing.

Buying second-hand can be a splendid way to get value by spending less.[7] In reality, buying new has two great disadvantages.

(1) The price is often based on production and distribution costs and profit margins, not real market value.

(2) Anything you buy new becomes second-hand quickly. This is most evident when buying a car, and it's been true for decades that when you buy a new car and drive it around the block, it immediately loses one-third of its value. Actually, what it loses is one-third of *its market price* in inflated dollars. It will still get you there and back as well as a car with no miles on it.

Often, it's possible to get great savings in second-hand clothing. An asking price of one-tenth of the new, store-bought price is typical. Garage sales are good sources of second-hand clothing, as it's often possible to find items in excellent condition.

Flea markets and second-hand stores are also good sources, perhaps even better because they save the buyer a lot of running around.[8] This is a real saving. Going to a Goodwill store, where you can find exactly what you need in several categories in one trip, is a better deal than the hit-or-miss of driving around to a hundred garage sales. You pay more, but save a lot of time, gasoline, and wear-and-tear on the car.

Barter is yet another well-known technique, one that requires no further explanation. It's a growing practice in this country, as a part of "Guerrilla Economics."[9]

What people throw away is surprising.[10] What's equally surprising is the value of items to be found at "dumps." Often, people receive gifts they don't want or simply get tired of something they bought and throw it away.[11]

We see, therefore, that it's possible to get a lot more mileage from money than most of us do. Savings on expenditures are not only real savings, but are not taxable. Furthermore, some people do so well at this that they can commit the sacrilege of taking a lower-paying, or part-time job, which cuts the tax bite.

This last part is the real benefit of smart economics. While we can devote many pages to specific techniques of earning tax-free income, and analyze patterns of spending, there's no way to measure the value of free time, or relief from the pressure of a job.

Many people suffer from their jobs. Overwork is a real cause of illness, and stress from work causes heart attacks, high blood pressure, and other disorders. This is not counting illnesses and deaths from radioactivity, asbestos, and other industrial hazards.

It does no good to say that "Type A" people suffer more coronaries than do others. If you're a Type A person, the easiest course is to remove the cause of the stress.

Many people, although not afflicted by physical illness, do suffer psychologically from work. This is so common that we don't often notice it, and take it for granted. The boredom of spending five days a week in the same place, doing the same work with the same people, takes its toll. The harmful effects of abuse suffered on the job are intangible, but real.

The time it takes to commute, without pay, is taken from our lives. The anxiety we suffer, if we have jobs that produce anxiety, wears us down.

Enough people are "wage slaves" that this is a serious public-health problem, although the government won't admit it. The Occupational Safety and Health Administration concentrates on obvious physical hazards, such as dangerous materials, and ignores the psychological hazards of wage labor. To question the negative psychological effects of work would bring into question the very value of the "system," and the powers-that-be don't want than.

Anyone who has worked for a living knows, either from his own experience or that of fellow employees or friends, that the psychological hazards are more severe than the physical ones. Eating your heart out for a raise, the strain of office and shop politics, the endless waiting for a promotion, are just a few of the common stresses. The day-to-day hassle of being an employee, the petty aggravations, all take their toll. This is one reason why "happy hours" and "liquid lunches" are so popular.

Psychologists are part of the establishment, and they focus on blaming the individual, not the system, for mental problems that lead to alcohol abuse and other chemical ingestions. They rarely admit that the pressures of the job can and do unhinge their patients. This leads to increased pressure on the people who are suffering the most, as they are coerced into re-examining their pasts to uncover the cause and roots of their "problems."

There are simpler solutions. *Reduce the pressure. Reduce the dependency on wage-earning. Seek the job satisfaction that self-employment affords. Find the freedom that comes with being your own boss.* Often, a change of scene will abolish the symptoms. Taking up the rural life, although it has its problems, is one way to do this.[12]

These are not solutions that we'll hear from psychologists. The few companies that offer "employee counseling" programs have only one end: to help the employee "adjust" and become a better employee. The company's interest comes first, last and always. *No counselor will advise an employee to strike out on his own.* He knows on which side his bread is buttered.

Finding answers to your problems is up to you. Your boss won't help you. Often, nobody else will help you. This is frustrating, and it's a lonely struggle. But this isn't all bad, because when you do find a solution, you'll have the satisfaction of knowing that you did it on your own, and in that way have regained some control over your life.

There is no total or ideal solution, only a number of partial ones. Earning extra income is one way to cope. Reducing expenses is another way. If you're lucky or skillful enough to make the two meet, so that you can work less because you can get along on your lower income, the whole will be greater than the sum of its parts.

NOTES

1. *How To Survive Without A Salary,* Charles Long, New York, Sterling Publishing Co., 1981, pp. 11-12.

2. *Ibid.,* p. 13.

3. *Ibid.,* pp. 18-19.

4. *Ibid.,* pp. 31-47.

5. *Ibid.,* pp. 48-71.

6. *Ibid.,* p. 94.

7. *Ibid.,* pp. 118-139.

8. *Ibid.,* pp. 134-137.

9. *Ibid.*, p. 167.

10. A "sanitation worker" told of the many usable items he found in making the rounds collecting garbage. He was not too proud to take the more valuable ones home to his family, saving the surplus to renovate and sell to friends and neighbors. These items included appliances such as toasters and TVs, toys, clothing, and even canned food.

11. In the experience of the author, going out to the desert each week has produced:

A five-dollar bill, probably lost.

Countless coins, also lost.

A jar of caviar.

A new air conditioner.

Thousands of pounds of aluminum cans, for recycling.

At least twenty thousand fired cartridge cases, for reloading.

Several boxes of unfired ammunition.

Assorted lumber, for the fireplace or for casual construction.

Assorted hardware, including nails, screws, washers, locks, etc.

Packs of cigarettes. This is a bad habit. Why pay to give yourself cancer? Pick them up free.

Assorted medical supplies.

A pocketknife in good condition.

Spray cans of paint.

This is only a partial list, from memory. In reality, there was a lot more out there, ignored because it was unneeded.

12. *Living Off The Country,* John L. Parker, Ontario, CA, Bookwork Publishing Company, 1978. This is a comprehensive,

no-nonsense book about the thrills and the problems that accompany a rural lifestyle. It suggests many ways of earning money from rural occupations, most of them centered around livestock and agriculture.

The advantages of rural life are many. On a farm, you save money by growing your food, instead of buying. You also have housing, and save on utilities.

With the rising cost of energy, saving on electricity becomes more important. In the city, you depend on it for transportation, even to run the elevator in your apartment house. You literally can't do without it, as using a fire for heating is forbidden in cities with pollution-control laws.

Water, basic to life, costs in the city. Having your own well can make you independent of the water company.

Clothing, important for many who work in the city, is less of a problem on a farm, where jeans and boots are more useful than a three-piece suit.

Even basic sanitation is simpler and cheaper. A septic tank or outhouse eliminates the need to pay a plumber forty or more dollars an hour.

Finally, there is the air. The government hasn't yet put a tax on it, but in the city breathing is hazardous to your health.

15

Compromise Solutions

No one person can follow all the suggestions and plans in these "Guerrilla Capitalist" volumes. No single person can have all the skills listed for these ideas, nor the clientele.

Although various underground money-making plans are worthwhile, they take time to carry out. Some of the ideas may be too bold for some people. Other people may simply not have the time. A person with a large family, and consequently heavy responsibilities, may not feel like taking risks, and may also not have the time, because he's already working two jobs to put bread on the table.

There are no perfect solutions — all have their benefits and disadvantages. Nevertheless, the worst case of all is the wage-earner who has income taxes and other deductions amputated before he even sees his paycheck, under the bland name of "withholding."

For the person who has difficulty taking long steps, or whose time is very limited, there are still some steps to take. These are the compromise solutions, efforts that involve little risk, and which bring limited benefits.

Let's examine the exact meaning of "lifetime benefits." First, any plan which promises you unlimited wealth is unrealistic. Any plan which claims you can make a certain sum each week is also unrealistic, because this is impossible to predict. However, we can say a "limited benefit" means you're better off than before. Often, this is enough. A person whose take-home pay is two hundred and fifty dollars a week may feel this isn't enough to take care of his and his family's needs. He doesn't need a take-home of two thousand dollars a week to fulfill his needs. Perhaps another fifty will do it.

People's needs aren't absolute, and neither are their ways of fulfilling them. There is a great middle ground between the wealthiest and the poorest, and most of us can fit comfortably at some point in the middle ground. Most of the time, a slight increase in real income will do it. As many financial problems are not large, just small creeping ones, a modest solution is enough.

For example, all of us are affected by inflation. Each year, we see our purchasing power decline, if we don't get an increase in income that overcomes both inflation and the "bracket creep." Someone who doesn't get a raise one year, while inflation eats up five percent of his income, doesn't need to double his income to keep up. He needs only to increase his real, after-tax income by five percent to break even. Anything more is gravy.

With this in mind, let's examine several ways to increase real income without paying taxes on it.

One way is to refuse raises. What? Is this man mad? Refuse a raise when I can't get along with what I'm earning now?

Okay, okay, calm down, and let's look at the problem with raises. If you get enough of a raise, you will find yourself in a higher tax bracket, which will eat up more of what you earn, and if you're right on the borderline between two tax brackets, may leave you with less take-home pay than before. This has happened to enough people to make raises bad risks, unless they're very generous.

Labor unions know this. So do employers. That's why there's so much emphasis on fringe benefits today. They're not taxable. When the time for a raise comes around, try to get another fringe benefit instead. You'll like it, and the boss, who has to pay proportionally to your income on Social Security, will like it, too. Let's look at possible fringe benefits and see what you might consider.

Medical insurance. Many employees don't have medical insurance. If you don't have this as a fringe benefit, you have to do without, or provide your own from the money you get after taxes. Oh, yes, it's "deductible," but that does not mean the IRS will refund you the money you spend on it, or on any other medical expenses. A deduction is not the same as a tax credit. A tax credit means you take what you're allowed directly off the tax you owe. A deduction means that you take it off your taxable income, and if you're in the thirty percent tax bracket, you only get thirty cents on the dollar. Persuading the boss to buy you medical insurance can save you a lot of money, because it's not taxable at all, and he can deduct it on his tax return just as he does your pay and other business expenses.

Vacations. This doesn't put any more money in your pocket, but it does give you more free time, during which you can work at something else, unless you feel you really need the rest and recuperation. If you get a one-week vacation per year now, ask for more, unless there's something else you'd prefer.

Lunch. Many companies have cafeterias, where employees can buy their lunch at moderate prices. In effect, these are non-profit restaurants run by the employers. A benefit you might request is a free lunch instead of a raise. Put it to the boss this way: It costs him at least five dollars a week per person to run the cafeteria. If you're up for a ten dollar a week raise, he can instead provide free lunches and pocket the difference. Everybody benefits.

Company car. This privilege, usually reserved for executives, might apply to you, if you're a trusted blue-collar employee. Ask your boss if, instead of a raise, you can take the truck home each night, bringing it back in the morning.

85

To persuade him to do this, you have to be reliable, with an excellent record of attendance. He'll need that truck in the morning, and if you don't bring it in, even if you have a legitimate excuse such as illness, he'll be seriously inconvenienced.

This can save you big bucks. Have you considered what your car costs to run per mile? A figure of twenty cents a mile is low. Even the IRS allows that on tax returns, and they're not overly generous. If you drive to work ten miles each way, a reasonable figure, you spend an extra four dollars each day to do so. It multiplies out to twenty dollars a week. This means twenty dollars after taxes, which means that you have to earn *more* than that in gross pay. Suggesting to the boss that letting you have the vehicle will be equal to you of a **twenty-five (roughly) dollar per week raise will be appealing, especially as he won't have to lay out that much cash. Sweeten the pot by promising to keep it washed.**

This last point brings us to a discussion of negotiation. Successful negotiation is the key to coming to an agreement. Many people forget this. We see a number of books dealing with techniques of negotiation on the shelves. Whoever the author might be, and whatever approach he takes, the basic principle is the same: Both parties must get something out of the deal.

One foreman complained: "These people come in here, and it's always the same. 'Stick 'em up!'" He was somewhat emotional about it, but his point was clear. He resented his employees' asking him for raises without offering anything in return. The company didn't earn unlimited income, and the front office only gave him a certain budget within which to work.

When you negotiate with your employer, decide beforehand how to present your proposal so he sees immediately that he gets something out of it, too. Make it a trade, not a one-way demand. Even if he refuses, he'll be more likely to give you a good reason, or even come back with a counter-proposal which you might find acceptable.

Employers pay close attention to an employee's attitude. They like one who thinks of the company's welfare as well as his own. They resent those who seek only what they can take from the company. Employers have their blind spots. They often see themselves as very generous and their employees as ungrateful wretches.

This is why you should make it a firm rule to offer your boss something in return when you ask for anything. The message you'll get across to him is that you're looking out for him, too.

Trade-outs. This is an often unexplored way of getting extra compensation without giving the IRS a chance at it. We've already seen, in previous volumes, how individuals arranged such deals for themselves.

What does your company make? Can you use any of it, and would you accept some instead of a raise?

This can work anytime, not just when you feel you're up for a raise. A good example is overtime. Employers hate overtime. Suggest to your employer that he might pay you for overtime in trade. This gives both sides several advantages, the first one being that it keeps the transaction "off the books."

Even if both sides charge each other "full list," with you expecting goods equivalent to what you accrue at time-and-a-half, and he charges you what he charges his customers, not his cost, you both benefit. It'll work expecially well for you if he's a manufacturer, distributor or wholesaler, not a retailer.

If, for example, your employer deals in food, it's obvious that you can use some for yourself and your family. There might be a problem, though, if he deals in hard goods such as binoculars. Although he might be willing to trade you a pair or two in return for some labor, if you ask for more than that it will occur to him that you're selling them to your friends, and have set yourself up in competition with him. He'll find that unacceptable. If he manufactures or deals in controlled substances, such as explosives or certain drugs, a trade-out might not be possible, and could even be illegal.

Employers sometimes ask some of their employees to take on tasks that are out of their regular work. This is a good opportunity to ease into contract labor.

16

Gain Experience — Work Free

There's a popular belief, encouraged by many magazine, newspaper and television ads, that you have to enroll in a special training school to learn a skill. Many people, lured by the promise of big money, pay large fees to these schools and are later disappointed. They often find that they can't do the work, or that the course is inadequate, or that, upon graduation, there's little demand for their new-found skills.

There's a far less expensive way to learn a skill. Approach the owner of a business and offer to work for free, in return for instruction. This is a far better method, for these reasons:

(1) You don't lay out any money, which keeps your investment minimal, until you decide that you want to work in the field.

(2) You learn at your own pace, putting in the hours you feel you can spare. With no formal schedule, you don't have to keep up with a class, and can adjust your pace to suit your needs and schedule.

(3) There's no overestimating the value of on-the-job training. You not only learn the skill itself, you learn what the market is like in your area, and the special conditions and problems that affect people in the field. You get practical experience in dealing with customers, learn which are the

credit risks, and all of the many details you can only get through O.J.T.

(4) Rather than getting the overly optimistic propaganda put out by a school that earns its money by giving you instruction, you find out what it's *really* like, the problems *and* the drawbacks. As an unpaid employee, you'll enjoy special status, as the boss will not have to worry about your trying to get a raise, or other concessions. He may even take you to lunch or supper a few times, a nominal reward for your services.

(5) Often, people feel flattered that someone shows enough regard for their skills that they seek to learn from them. In such cases, they tend to open up more, to be more frank, and reveal the real conditions of the work instead of presenting the public relations view. The owner of the business will probably tell you candidly about the best sources of supplies, the ones which offer the greatest discounts, and the ones which usually keep a good stock on hand. This is up to date trade information and is invaluable to someone starting out.

There can be problems, though. Don't try to apprentice yourself to a locksmith, unless he knows you well. He would suspect the motives of anyone walking in off the street and offering to work at this sensitive job free.

You might run into an exploitative employer, or one who feels that free labor is worth exactly what he pays for it. If so, you'll find yourself being used as a "gofer," instead of being allowed to work at the trade. If you find that you spend more than half your time making deliveries, and getting coffee and donuts for "the boys," it's time to leave.

If you're lucky enough to have a friend in the business, you can learn a lot, both from "hands on" training and informally, listening to his candid comments after hours.

17

More Underground Economy People

Frank works in a gun store. He also teaches shooting on the side. Although not a top competitive shooter, he's more than good enough to teach people the basics of armed defense, which has little to do with competitive shooting, anyway. He seeks his prospects among his customers, and convinces novices who buy firearms for home defense that owning the weapons is only half the story. He and a partner take small, informal groups out to a deserted area each weekend and give them a basic course in how to handle and fire their weapons. Payment is usually in cash, and the few checks they get they "launder," either cashing them at the banks they were drawn on or endorsing them to others to pay off bills.

Ellen lives in one of the "old neighborhoods" in an Eastern city. Most of the people in her neighborhood live in apartments, and are "business couples" with both husband and wife working. Ellen decided to earn extra money by taking in washing, saving her customers the trouble of taking their wash to the laundromat and having to wait for it, then folding their laundry and re-packing it. She inquired door-to-door, and the response was enough to get her started. She then put up a card describing her services in the local market, and even on the bulletin board of the laundromat on the corner! As Ellen lives in a house, with a washer and dryer in the basement, she finds it easy and profitable to work her business in with the rest of her housework. On particularly busy days, she employs her oldest boy to deliver to and pick up from her customers. She offers same-day service at no extra charge. If the customer delivers his or her laundry to her before eight in the morning, on the way to work, it is ready for pickup at five the same day. Ellen usually gets paid in cash, but the occasional checks she passes at the local market, as the owner has known her for years, and accepts her third-party checks without hassle or questions. This is a largely immigrant neighborhood, and many of the residents distrust and fear the authorities, which means that she has no reason to fear being denounced to the IRS.

Perry, a retired Secret Service Agent, has a generous government pension, and earns money on the side by providing "executive protection," the current term for bodyguarding, to select clients. Most of his assignments are short-term, guarding people who have received threats until their fears subside. He gets his business both by word-of-mouth and through referrals from a friend, another retired Secret Service Agent, who runs a private guard agency. When his friend gets a request that his "rent-a-cops" can't handle, he calls in Perry. As most of the clients pay by check, Perry "launders" these through his friend, and they split the profits. Perry gets many fringe benefits through these contacts. Many of his clients travel extensively, taking Perry with them. Perry knows that in most cases the threats are only imaginary, and feels safe visiting foreign places with the clients paying the freight. As the executive protection agent must stay close to the protectee, Perry gets the benefits of staying in expensive hotels and eating at the same expensive restaurants his clients do. This sideline pays for some travel that Perry otherwise wouldn't be able to afford. The risk isn't as great as readers of sensational popular novels would believe. In reality, the main emphasis in executive protection is avoidance, not gun battles, and Perry arranges for his clients' schedules and movements so as to minimize the risk of encountering a threat. In his career, both in the Secret Service and in private practice, he's never had a shootout. He feels confident of living to a ripe old age.

Madame Yvonne is a part-time underground seamstress catering to the Park Avenue trade, and she works out of her home. In New York, there are many custom dressmakers, skilled people who build dresses from scratch or alter store-bought ones, and they operate from locations with heavy overhead, as we'd expect from a high-rent district. Madame Yvonne learned her trade in France, where she was born, and her distinctive French accent gives her a prestigious aura with her clients. The prices she charges are significantly below those charged by the high-overhead custom alterers, and she keeps it all, tax-free. Using her young son to make pick-ups and deliveries, she turns over enough business to make it all worthwhile.

Mike owns his own garage, repairing foreign cars. With his partner, Steve, he also restores old and badly beat-up foreign classics. He gets spare parts at mechanic's discounts, which makes the proposition more attractive, and he doesn't even have to do all the work himself. He uses the old car projects as "fillers" when business is slow, and puts his mechanics to work on them. He gets discounts on painting, which he's not equipped to do. He already had a going business, and all his tools and facilities are written off as part of the business. For him, it's pure profit.

Janice, a housewife, had to give up her job as a pet groomer to take care of her new son. This requires her to stay at home all day, except for shopping and visiting, when she takes her son with her. In the search for extra cash, she had an easy start. In her job, she'd built up many personal contacts, and had a clientele that liked her work. Many clients, bringing their pets for grooming, would ask specifically for her. Janice planned ahead. She built up a list of names and telephone numbers of clients who liked her work. When she was pregnant, and ready to leave her job, she had some business cards printed, giving her home address. During her last weeks, she handed them out to her list of clients, adding verbally that she'd give their pets the same care for less money. She could afford to do this as she anticipated no overhead. Planning to work at home, she already had her personal set of tools. Not having to rent a store, she has practically no expenses. Her husband, George, built her some holding pens in the back yard, where she keeps pets waiting for her care or for their owners to pick them up.

Rich and Ron own an exterminating business. They have made a comfortable living from it for years. One reason they find it comfortable is that they also have some clients on the side. They bill their big commercial clients in the normal way, sending an invoice at the end of the month. Some of their private clients, however, get a special deal. These are friends, to whom they make the offer: "Pay us cash, keep it off the books, and we give you a good discount for your trouble."

Fred was an early retiree, having made his "pile" legitimately, and had many tens of thousands in the bank. Realizing that inflation was eating up most of what he earned in interest, and taxes taking the rest, he looked around for another way of investing. His nephew was a bright young man, who was seeking to open up a fried-chicken franchise, but lacked the money. The nephew was eating his heart out as an "assistant manager" of a fried-chicken franchise, and knew he was slaving away as a counter clerk for almost no money, despite the title. Fred, knowing the nephew was both capable and experienced, approached him with this offer: He'd give him the money to buy into a franchise. The money was a gift, not a loan, and there would be no paperwork recorded anywhere. In return, he simply wanted a percentage of the "take." The nephew would be able to earn enough to pay this percentage without strain every month, giving Fred a steady, untraceable retirement income. Fred found this worked so well that he did it with several other bright young businessmen types he knew, and soon had a totally underground income that gave him a better lifestyle than he could have earned otherwise.

Jerry operates a tire store, and he saves the wheel weights that come off customers' rims. Instead of selling them to a scrap dealer, he sells them, in small amounts, to several friends who are into reloading and cast their own bullets using wheel weights as a base. He gets more money from his friends than he would from a dealer, and his friends don't have to buy carload lots as they would at a dealer's. They pay cash, and Jerry doesn't enter the sales on his books.

Len is a farmer who collects extra income during the hunting season. He charges hunters a small fee for hunting on his land. The hunters pay it willingly, as Len's farm is conveniently close to the city and they know they have a certain amount of protection while on Len's land. The game wardens don't patrol private property in the same way they oversee state land, and minor violations usually go undetected. Len, of course, doesn't report the fees on his tax return.

Rick works as a photographer for a large and prestigious museum. Museum pay is not the best, and Rick has a sideline, using the barber training he picked up earlier in life. He cuts hair for his fellow employees during lunch and breaks, doing a fairly good, but not fancy job at less than half the going rate in barbershops. His investment in tools was minimal, since he had them left over from when he'd worked as a barber. He is able to use a straight-backed chair in his darkroom, and sweeping up the hair afterwards is not a serious problem because of the tile floor. Payment is always in cash, which he pockets, undisclosed to the IRS.

Ron is a homosexual, and owns a two-bedroom house. He rents his spare bedroom, finding tenants through a gay room-mate service. Although he doesn't have personal relationships with his "room-mates," he finds it comfortable to have people like him renting, because it avoids embarrassment. The extra, undeclared income helps him sustain the lifestyle he likes. He thinks that, although he's a city worker and not underpaid, the tax bite on his official salary is large enough.

18

Work at Home

This is a very old idea, older than most countries, and the basis of "cottage industries." Today it has a new meaning because of some provisions of the Internal Revenue Code.

If you've decided to reduce your tax bite by legal means, opening up a business in your home is one way of increasing your deductions. Another way is to bring work home with you, if your job allows this.

Each has its advantages and disadvantages. Let's take the last one first, because it's quicker to lay out.

Bringing work home is common, and it's foolproof. It depends on your occupation, of course. Some are just not adaptable. Others are.

Sam, a psychiatrist, had it made. He converted his garage to an office, and saw patients there during the evenings. This meant that both his and his wife's Cadillacs had to stand in the driveway, but Sam didn't mind. The extra deduction allowed him more money to buy another Cadillac for his daughter.

Ken, a commercial artist, brought home work with him from the agency where he worked. A corner of his bedroom was set up as a studio, complete with drawing board and art supplies. He had to clean up his act in recent years, because the IRS, aware of this dodge, stipulated that to qualify as a deduction, the entire room must be devoted for this task, and not used for anything else.

THE HOME BUSINESS

Roughly the same principles apply to the home business as to a free-standing one. It must make a profit, at least to endure the long run. It must build up a clientele, if it depends on repeat business and not one-shots.

Clientele is very important. One-shots, such as selling vacuum cleaners door-to-door and keeping one room at home for inventory, is very volatile and unstable. Anyone selling vacuum cleaners needs to hustle for each sale, week after week, and work hard to see fresh people each day to find possible buyers. Repeat business enables slowing down on selling effort, and re-directing the time to producing and servicing, which are usually more profitable.

One word of warning regarding clients: Be careful! Depending on the type of business and the locale, a new business can attract deadbeats, who can't get credit anywhere else in town and swarm around a new business like killer sharks, hoping the new proprietor won't be in business for long.

The same basic rule regarding taxes applies to the home business as to the hobby turned into a business. The IRS will scrutinize it very carefully, and it must show a profit over a period, or the IRS will disallow it. Generally, if it goes for three years without showing a profit, the IRS will clamp down hard.

With these basics laid out, we can turn to the characteristics a home business should have to serve as a tax shelter.

It should be work you do at home. Modeling is out, although you may work out of your home. Your actual work is off the premises, and whatever fee you charge, you'll have to pay part of it in taxes.[1]

Heavy manufacturing is out, as is anything requiring elaborate, expensive, or noisy special equipment. There are zoning laws, and it's pointless to try to evade one set of laws while laying yourself open to others.

"Make-money-at-home" schemes are not really that, but just systems for the advertiser to make money off you. Start your own business, not a branch of someone else's.

Generally, anything that is intellectual and creative will serve as a home business. It may require some equipment, such as a camera, but it's not heavy equipment and doesn't make noise enough to be conspicuous.

Model-making for architects is one craft that pays well if you develop the right contacts.[2] Model-making skills are not exotic talents, just careful work and craftsmanship, and it is a good choice for a home business.

Art of any sort is a natural for working at home. A commercial artist can free-lance for advertising agencies.[3] It seems easier than it really is, though. There's a special hazard connected to working for or with ad agencies, which the books don't tell you. Advertising people are flaky. You may get an assignment from one, and find when it's almost finished that it has to be changed so extensively that you have to start over. Short and unreasonable deadlines are another problem. People in the "ad biz" are supreme egotists, and think that anything is possible if they command it. You will find yourself working late into the night to meet a deadline if you lay yourself open to this. Finally, and perhaps decisively, ad agencies are typically deadbeats. The best of them pay very slowly, and you'll be carrying them for a long time, (90 days is a good average) before you see your money.

Free-lancing of any sort[4] that you can do at home is worthwhile, if you have the skill. Many people feel very insecure with this prospect, preferring to have one or two solid accounts, but this is a trap. Having only one or two accounts makes you a "captive shop." It's almost like having a regular job. It seems secure, but actually you have all your eggs in one or two baskets. If you lose the account, for whatever reason, you're in trouble.

Captive shops suffer from another problem that comes with this. The big account knows his power, knows the captive shop needs him more than he needs it, and often makes unreasonable demands, sometimes being crude enough to use the fear technique: "if you can't do it, I'll find someone who will."

Spreading the business around provides insulation from these problems. It multiplies the chances of running into bad clients, and slow payers, but these undesirable features tend to average out. It makes it much easier to drop a truly bad account.

Light mechanical work is another possibility. Watch repair, appliance repair,[5] and other light repair work which you can do at home without disturbing the neighbors are suited for this purpose.

Crafts of any sort are risky. These include jewelry,[6] glass blowing,[7] and candle holders[8]. Such crafts are drags on the market, and unless you already have a market lined up, stay away from them. You'll eat your heart out trying to sell your works.

It's much the same with fine arts of any sort. Traditionally, artists starve, partly because of uncertain demand, and partly because paintings and sculptures consume so much time that people won't pay prices that provide a living.

Writing free-lance[9] is fairly secure, if you have the ability and are able to start at it part-time, working up your clientele. Luck helps in getting started, but in the long run your ability, or lack of it, will be decisive.

Working at home is worth the effort, if you're lucky enough to do it and you approach it in the right way. Once you decide that tax relief is possible by changing your

100

occupation of lifestyle, you can work out your step-by-step plan. You'll either phase yourself into it, or jump in with both feet, depending on your occupation, skill, responsibilities, and most importantly, your personality.

NOTES

1. *The #1 Home Business Book,* George and Sanda Delany, Cockeysville, MD, Liberty Publishing Company, 1982, p. 67.

2. *Ibid.,* p. 64.

3. *Ibid.,* p. 65.

4. *Ibid.,* pp. 67, 68, 79, and 81, for a start.

5. *Ibid.,* p. 127.

6. *Ibid.,* p. 92.

7. *Ibid.,* p. 91.

8. *Ibid.,* p. 88.

9. *Ibid.,* pp. 157-159.

19

Contract Labor

There's not much difference between a wage-earning employee and a contract employee with regard to the nature of the work, but there's a big difference in the ways they're paid. A wage-earner is a legal employee, working for an hourly or weekly wage, and is subject to withholding on his paycheck. The contract employee does approximately the same work, but is paid hourly by the "job," and gets to keep it all. Of course, he must pay his taxes, but the legal responsibility is his, not his employer's.

Let's take a close look at exactly what a contract employee is, both the practical definitions and the IRS's. The contract employee is not committed to the job or the company. He accrues no seniority, gets no fringe benefits, and his employment lasts only for the life of the "contract," which often is verbal. In short, he's nominally a temporary employee, although his term of employment in practice may be longer than some "permanent" employees laid off when the workload slows down. He collects his full contracted fee, without any withholding. The word "fee," is very important. He charges a fee, because he's self-employed. He bills the company, and is not on the regular payroll.

Some of the occupations in which it's possible to work on contract are:

Accountant	Janitor
Appraiser	Machinist
Beautician	Nurse
Broker	Photographer
Copywriter	Printer
Dog trainer	Rental Agent
Exterminator	Salesperson
Gardener	Typesetter
Instructor	Window Washer

The IRS has some guidelines for determining whether an individual is a contract employee or not. The most important ones are:

Billing. Does the contract employee charge by the hour or by the job? A fee is more impressive than a listed hourly wage.

Regularity. Does the contractor work nine-to-five hours? Does he punch a time card? If so, he's an employee.

Other contracts. Is the contractor also doing work for other companies, or is this one his only "employment?"

Location of work. Does the contractor perform his work on the company's premises, using the company's tools and equipment, or does he work at home, or use his own tools?

Supplies. Does the contractor provide his own supplies?

Length of employment. Temporary short-term, or long-term semi-permanent?

Separate business checking account?

There are other criteria, but they are not as vital. In practice, it's safe if you cover your bases by doing even occasional work for another firm, to demonstrate that you're not an "employee" of the one which gets most of your time.

The advantages of being a contractor are immediate and significant. One of the most important is the paycheck you get is intact.

This does not absolve you from the obligation to pay taxes, however. You have to keep your own books, and send in a quarterly estimated tax payment. However, while you're earning, you deposit your checks in your business account and collect the interest on the money. The IRS, even if it gives you a refund at the end of the year, does not pay you interest on the money it held. This can make a significant difference. The government invests the money it collects, until it needs it, but it doesn't give you even a share of the interest of dividends earned on the money it refunds you. By even a mundane investment, such as in a bank account that pays eight percent, you'll collect interest on it, which is better than nothing, even if that interest is taxable.

The benefits to the employer are also immediate and significant. He doesn't have to keep a payroll record on you, calculate your withholding, and issue you a check each week. In fact, he may ask you to bill him once a month, to save him time in writing checks. It also absolves him from paying matching Social Security tax on your labor. You're no longer covered by Workmen's Compensation or Unemployment Insurance, which means he saves there, too. If he has a pension plan for his employees, he'll drop you from it. The deal is attractive to him. He withholds roughly three dollars from the pay of a ten-dollar an hour employee, and has to pay yet more himself, depending on the fringe benefits.

Since he doesn't have to pay the additional expenses on your work, you can ask him to pay you more. It'll be a net gain for both of you. He'll also find it attractive that he's not committed to paying for forty hours a week. He'll simply call you as he needs you. This can be good or bad for you, depending on how you handle it.

If you're working for minimum wage, or slightly above it, you'll lose if you become a contract employee. If you're a skilled tradesman, you'll definitely gain.

As a self-employed person, you can deduct your mileage to and from work. This adds up to a lot at the end of the year.

Even in a city where it doesn't pay to drive, you can deduct your commuting costs, if you take public transportation. We earlier examined a reasonable figure for mileage, and found that ten miles each way, each day, costs four dollars for a five-day week. Assuming fifty work weeks a year, that multiplies out to two hundred dollars. Deducting and getting back thirty cents on the dollar makes a difference to you of sixty dollars a year. You'll also be able to deduct more mileage. As a self-employed person, the trip to the bank to deposit your check will be deductible, as will any trip connected with your business.

You can deduct eating out, unlike an employee. If you incur any legal fees as a contractor, they're also deductible. Any business license you need also comes off your taxes.

Generally, you can deduct more for tools, machinery, postage, and telephone than you could if you were an employee. Furthermore, if you take work home with you, and use one room of your home exclusively for that, you can deduct your rent or mortgage and utilities in proportion to what you use.

Various insurance plans to which you may subscribe become deductible. In short, you have available to you far more deductions than you did as an employee.

Not only will you have to manage your money very well, but your time. You may not have the security of forty hours per week work from an account, and in fact it's better if you don't. Working full-time for one company makes you seem an employee to the IRS, and it may disallow your status.

It's better if you have several accounts, for these reasons:

(1) It establishes you as a truly self-employed person, very important if you're ever audited.

(2) It gives you more security. The worst possible case is to have all of your eggs in one basket, depending on one job. Many people think that a "steady job" means security, but in fact many jobs are not "steady" at all. Even the largest companies have layoffs, with thousands of employees

suddenly out in the cold. Even civil service jobs aren't secure, as the recent events in New York show us. Having income from more than one source means that if one dries up, you haven't lost all your income, and you can use the free time to seek more accounts.

You have to cope with being out in the cold. You won't have employee benefits, but it's not as bad as it seems at first. You can provide medical insurance for yourself, and still come out ahead. You ought to be aware, though, that individual medical insurance costs more than does a group plan of the sort employers have. As for unemployment insurance, the payments are so low that even a part-time job pays more. In fact, you can get along better by working some small contracts than if you were on unemployment.

This brings us to managing your time. What do you do during your off-hours? If you don't need any more money, you can rest. You can also use the time to sell yourself, seeking new accounts. The problem with accounts is that they don't necessarily last. Companies do go out of business, do relocate, do have a slow periods, and these affect contract employees as well as regular ones. It's a mistake to assume that your main account will be with you forever.

You're even better off without a main account, but a slew of small ones. That way, no account can hold you in bondage. The example of one small businessman makes the point.

Joe had set up his own graphic arts shop, and his main account was a large department store nearby. This account gave him eighty percent of his business, and he knew he couldn't survive without it, as his other accounts were too small to pay even his overhead. The problem was that the head of the advertising department knew it too, and had the personality of a tyrant. This executive habitually cracked the whip, making unreasonable demands, knowing Joe could not refuse. Joe tried half-heartedly to get other accounts, but was not able to build up his other business enough to enable him to get out from under.

Possibly the greatest benefit of being self-employed is psychological. You do your work, whatever it may be, without having someone over you. While it's true that you have to be responsive to your accounts' needs, and keep them happy, you can deal with them more on equal terms than you were able to as an employee and subordinate. Simply, you get more respect.

In dealing with your accounts, you'll find they won't show you the resentful treatment many of them have for their employees. They'll see you as a fellow businessman, one who is on the same side of the fence as they are, instead of an opponent in the labor-management struggle.

The question of loyalty also comes in. As an employee, your boss may resent your working part-time for another company, especially if the other is a competitor. He'll label it a "conflict of interest" if he wishes, and can hassle you for it. Some companies oblige new employees, as a condition of employment, to sign forms that they will not work for any competitor for as long as they work for that company.

Some employers are very possessive about their workers, forgetting that they don't own them. As an independent contractor, you'll be free of this hassle, and will be able to contract with a number of other companies. Moreover, the owners won't expect that sort of blind loyalty from you, as a rule, and if one does make such an unreasonable demand on you, you'll be able to abandon the account, as long as he's not your main one.

While it's true that there are unreasonable and abusive people in every line of work, and that you'll find some of your customers to be that way, you're not in the terribly vulnerable position you'd be if you were bound to them for forty hours a week. You'll even be able to pick and choose your customers after a while, dropping the troublesome ones and staying with those who treat you well.

Even the problem personalities won't seem as bad. You'll be able to console yourself with the knowledge that you have to see them only for a few hours per week, and pity their employees who are trapped and can't leave when one job is finished.

INCORPORATION

To incorporate or not? There are different opinions, and the proper course depends on your level of income. While it's true that incorporation definitely sets you up as an independent contractor with the IRS, it's also costly. Roughly, depending on the lawyer and the state, it costs from three to six hundred dollars to have a lawyer arrange for you to incorporate. There are kits out to permit you to incorporate for fifty dollars, but in a matter such as this, it's best to be cautious.

Generally, unless you earn fifty thousand dollars a year or more, it doesn't pay to incorporate. It seems prestigious, but the benefits are small. There are some tax advantages, such as paying the corporate tax rate instead of the individual tax rate of the sole proprietorship, but the cost of incorporation is an "overhead" that will eat up your tax saving below a certain income level. The best way to decide this is to ask your accountant, who is familiar with the laws in your state, and who knows your situation.

BEATING THE SYSTEM

One problem that arises with any sort of salary is the traceability through the worker's Social Security Number. We've seen how some avoid this by giving the employer a false Social Security Number, and how they can prolong the process before they move on to avoid an IRS investigation. Contracting offers another method of "beating the system."

Johnny hated the Internal Revenue Service, and took every opportunity he could to beat the system. Johnny was the owner of a small firm, and one of the devices he used to beat the system was to employ contract labor. Typically, he'd hire his friends, and arrange an unusual system of payment with them.

Johnny knew that, at the time, the Internal Revenue Code required him to send in a Form 1099 on each contractor to whom he paid more than six hundred dollars each year. Therefore, he listed them under assumed names, and falsified Social Security Numbers. On his books no contractor received over four hundred and fifty dollars, low enough to avoid arousing suspicion in case of an audit. When the inevitable inquiry regarding the Social Security Number arrived, Johnny could reply that he was unable to clarify the matter, as the employees had moved on without leaving a forwarding address.

He found that this system worked well, even in the eventuality of the rules being changed and his having to send in a Form 1099 on each one regardless of the amount. This also had the side-effect of degrading the IRS' performance, as they'd be kept busy chasing down non-existent people to collect taxes from them, a task which would overload even the most sophisticated computer. Johnny worked this system year after year, keeping the same faces in his shop, but on the books he had a column of names representing short-term contractors who left every couple of weeks.

A WIDESPREAD PRACTICE

How common is this? How many people evade paying taxes this way? The fact is that nobody knows, although it's possible to make an estimate by indirect means. The estimate, by whatever methods, is bound to be inaccurate because the government's figures don't cover the whole realm of working for a living. For example, adding up the people employed and declaring taxes and Social Security payments can show the number doing this, and subtracting this figure from the available work force can give a very rough figure. One problem with this method is that many people, contractors, are not listed in the official figures used in deriving the employement rate.

This is because of bureaucratic methods used to compile these figures. The official, documented wage-earners are the basis for further calculations. This number does not include the already self-employed, professionals and contractors. When an employee becomes unemployed, and applies for unemployment "benefits," he goes on another list, and remains there until he either finds employment or the state's benefit period expires. He may be working "on the side," as many do while collecting unemployment, but as this is undeclared work, it doesn't appear on any list.

A peculiar thing happens when the benefit period expires, and the unemployed person can no longer collect. The government loses interest in him. As it no longer collects taxes from him, or pays him subsistence, he doesn't matter anymore, and becomes a non-person. The compilers make the assumption that he's not working because he doesn't want to work, and delete him from their statistics. Strange, but true. He disappears from the official totals used in calculating the labor force and the unemployment rate. The information is available, but the government doesn't bother to pick it up.

Only the Internal Revenue Service remains interested. Its agents will "flag" anyone who fails to file a return that year. This, by itself, isn't significant. People fail to file for all sorts of legitimate reasons. They die. They move abroad. They become injured or ill and no longer able to work. They retire. Failure to file does not mean that there will immediately be an intensive search for the non-filer, although the IRS does try to maintain an image of terrifying efficiency and dogged, relentless pursuit of tax delinquents.

HOW TOMMY BEAT THE SYSTEM

Tommy lost his job in a mass layoff when his employer's lush government contract came to an end. There would be a six-month gap between Tommy's termination and his re-hiring when a new contract came through, and Tommy's first stop after getting his pink slip was at the unemployment office, where he registered for benefits.

A condition of registering for unemployment benefits is to also register with the state employment service, and to be willing and able to take employment in one's job category. Tommy knew that this was only a formality, as three thousand other machinists had been laid off on the same day and dumped into the labor pool. The staffers at the state employment service also knew this, and realized that the local economy would not be able to absorb three thousand machinists. In fact, all of the state personnel involved knew that the laid-off employees would be taking part-time and underground jobs while waiting for their company to hire them back. The state benefits were simply not enough to feed a family, make house and car payments, and meet the other expenses of daily living.

It's a characteristic of government employees that they follow the rules only enough to "cover their asses." They go through the formalities, in this case asking Tommy, "Are you looking for work?" and noting his answer in their records, only to avoid an accusation that they're neglecting their jobs. They follow the prescribed form, even if they know that it's utter nonsense. That's the way the "system" is, and there are few zealots.

Tommy, more canny than most, had a friend who owned a fast food stand, and who needed some temporary help. He went to work, although his hourly wage was not even in the same bracket as what he'd been earning. Added to the unemployment check, though, it enabled him to keep his head above water until he was able to find something better.

Tommy's father-in-law owned a tool and die company, and wanted to hire him as a salesman, not only because he had the technical knowledge, but because Tommy had a likeable personality and also had worked at several machine shops in the area. These were all actual or potential

111

customers. Tommy accepted the "old man's" offer, and they came to an agreement. Tommy would not be listed as an employee. He'd work on a commission basis, and the father-in-law would make out the checks in different names each time, as Tommy had a method of cashing them lined up.

Tommy quit his fast-food job, and was an immediate success in his new field. His commissions averaged slightly more than he'd been earning as a machinist, and the work was much easier. He collected commissions while continuing to collect unemployment, knowing that this was a violation. He also knew that the bureaucrats understood that remaining unemployed for a protracted period was not unusual in these circumstances, and they didn't aggressively follow up each case to ensure that they were looking for work.

Laundering the checks was an easy problem to solve. Tommy's neighbor owned a gas station, and was able to cash them for him, even under assumed names. As Tommy gave him all of his gasoline and repair business, and was able to bring the company car to him for service, this proved a mutually profitable arrangement. One important point is that they were good friends. Tommy felt able to confide in his neighbor without fear that he might turn him in out of spite or jealousy, as some tax informers do.

Once the unemployment benefit period ended, Tommy had to make an arrangement for continuing his profile with the IRS. He knew that not filing a return for that year would provoke an inquiry, because the IRS would be curious regarding how he was able to pay his bills and support his family with no income. Tommy knew that he'd have to emerge above-ground, at least partly, to avoid becoming the subject of an investigation. This was another important point. Tommy was not greedy. He knew when it was time to quit.

His father-in-law took him on officially as a salesman, and paid him a "draw," an advance against commissions. This gave him an official income to show to the IRS, keeping them happy, and offered an opportunity for extra tax-free income. Tommy was a very successful salesman, and improved as time went on and he became more familiar with his accounts. His father-in-law agreed that he'd arrange the books so that Tommy's commissions, on paper, would approximately balance his draw, set at an amount that would be credible to the IRS. The excess he paid by checks made out to other names, as before, enabling Tommy to cash them anonymously and get the best of both worlds.

WHY TOMMY SUCCEEDED
WHILE OTHERS HAVE FAILED

We see from Tommy's example that "beating the system" involves some discretion and a sense of proportion. It's more difficult to get away with concealing income for an unreasonably long time, especially if it is necessary to remain in the same location. Transients can and do conceal their incomes, and remain virtually untraceable, but a family man with a permanent address must be careful.

We also see the need for help from trustworthy associates. It's possible to go it alone, but it's much easier to have help. Involving others can be risky, but the key to reducing the risk is to make them parties to the enterprise. Tommy's neighbor, if ever the truth came out, would have a hard time explaining why he cashed checks from non-existent persons. Likewise, Tommy's father-in-law had to do some creative accounting with his books, and disclosures would have exposed him, too. In this case, every person involved had an interest in keeping it quiet.

TRANSIENTS

There are several million migrant workers and other transients in this country. Nobody knows how many, because they don't stay in one place long enough for the census to catch up with them.

Typically, these people are true "journeymen," day laborers, without long-term contracts, who get paid by the day, each day, unless there's a more permanent arrangement. Payment is necessarily in cash or barter. Sometimes, a hobo will trade a day's work for three meals and a bed. In other instances, there's a little money for him in the deal.

Migrant farm workers travel from state to state, taking their families with them, showing up to work at harvest time, then moving on to the next opportunity. These people are true nomads, with no fixed addresses, and sometimes not even birth certificates. The government knows that they exist, but can't identify them individually.

They don't have bank accounts, as their pay is too low to go beyond buying the immediate necessities, and for this and other reasons payment is almost always in cash. This makes it untraceable.

There are several reasons why transients often don't pay income taxes.

(1) With cash payment, transactions are hard to trace, and there's not even an endorsed check to tie the laborer to the payment.

(2) There's no check on true identity. The farm operator or his foreman doesn't care about the laborer's background. Transient labor is hired and fired on the spot, and the only consideration is whether the laborer does his job.

(3) Farm transients, as contract laborers, "take the money and run."

(4) Sometimes the government assists them in running. As many migrant workers are also immigrant workers, the Immigration and Naturalization Service and its police force, the U.S. Border Patrol, conduct periodic sweeps to find and deport illegal immigrants. The Border Patrol Officers round them up, load them on a bus, and conduct them over the border, out of reach of the IRS. This, incidentally, is an

excellent example of how different agencies of the government work at cross-purposes.

(5) Finally, the amount of money involved, although it comes to millions of dollars, is not very much when spread over millions of migrant workers. Internal Revenue Service agents work on a quota system. The most commonly accepted figure is that the Service considers an agent productive if he can recover one hundred dollars in taxes for each hour he spends working. Whatever the actual quota, it's obvious that recovering taxes from a person who is hard to trace and who can yield only a few dollars if caught is not a productive activity, by their reckoning. This also tells us why the segment of the population that typically is the most law-abiding and responsible, the wage-slave with a permanent address, is hit hardest by the IRS. He's the most vulnerable.

From the foregoing, we can build up a picture of how the "system" works, and how to take advantage of loopholes and weak points. For most, this will mean being very discreet and clever, accepting the limitations of a fixed address and depending on finesse, rather than being nomadic, to beat the system.

20

Door-To-Door Selling

This can be a money-maker, but only in certain instances. If you're thinking of this as a side-line, you must realize you'll be depending a lot on luck, and that generally the deck is stacked against you.

The first type of arrangement to consider is the dealership, which is basically a full-time occupation. You sign a contract with the parent company, and it specifies that you're an independent dealer. This means that you buy from them, at a discount, and sell to the customer at list, or whatever price you can get. In essence, you're self-employed, and the parent company has no responsibility towards you except to furnish you with the goods you buy.

You will have to give your Social Security number when you sign the contract, and the company will keep a record of what you buy from them. But you will keep your own records of what you sell and the prices you sell at, and since most of your customers will pay you cash, it is pretty much up to you what you report.

Generally, you have to invest several hundred dollars in a sales kit. In the case of Fuller Brush or Avon, you get a case and an assortment of the company's products to display as samples. The company will also sell you catalogs and small envelopes of its cosmetics and other products as giveaways.

In the case of a vacuum cleaner manufacturer, you'll have to buy a machine to use as a demonstrator.

The first decision for you is whether you want to sell big ticket or small ticket items. It's much harder to sell a machine costing several hundred dollars than it is a seven-dollar brush or broom, or a two-dollar tube of lipstick. The percentage of profit for you is high, running between 25% and 50%, but you'll sell fewer of the big items. The small ticket items sell faster, and you're not putting all your eggs in one basket. You can expect some income each week, although it may be small.

One serious problem for the newcomer is the allocation of "territories." Some companies lay out territories, exclusive dealerships in each geographical area. What this means for you is that the good territories are already taken, and you'll get one of the least profitable areas.

Despite the claims of your sales manager, who may tell you "It's not the bum territory, it's the bum in the territory," there are differences, and the experienced salesmen hold on to their territories, as they know when they've got good deals. Anyone entering a new territory should ask himself why the previous salesman left, and why it hasn't been taken by another salesman.

Basically, there can be two things wrong with a territory — poor sales and poor payment. In some territories, it's hard to make sales, either because the people have high sales resistance or because they're not at home most of the time. In others, the people have little money, and although a super-salesman can fill his book with orders, he finds it rough going when it comes time to collect the money.

Al, a new salesman, was allowed a territory all the other salesmen considered undesirable. However, he was a silver-tongued salesman, who from his first week managed to fill his order books with more orders than anyone else in the district. The sales manager was very proud of him, and invited him to stand up and speak at the monthly sales meetings. Al would get up and tell how he attained fabulous success by following the "company program" while the experienced salesmen listened quietly, reserving judgment. Al found he couldn't collect on more than a small percentage of his sales, because most of the residents in his territory were on welfare or unemployment compensation, and simply didn't have the money. He was gone within three months.[1]

The second type of arrangement is the part-time affair, in which you're recruited by a full-time dealer who sells to you at a smaller discount than he gets from the company. You work after-hours or on weekends, take the orders, pass on your orders to your dealer, and pay him for them. The dealer gets an "over-ride" on what you sell, because of the difference in discounts. The advantage is that this is an informal arrangement, and the parent company has no record of you and your sales.

This can be a worthwhile arrangement for you, partly because you're only dipping your toe into the water and not investing much time and money in it, and partly because there's a better chance of working a good territory. Another fact to consider is that, if the products are in demand, you can sell to your friends and fellow-employees, offering them a discount, and still make money with very little work.

While the territories laid out by the company can be bad or good, they're usually not uniform, because in each territory there are good blocks and bad blocks. If there are too many bad blocks, the full-time salesman can't earn enough to live, and that's the end of the story. The part-timer, however, will quickly learn which are good and which are bad, and can get a high return on his time by concentrating on the good ones, ignoring the bad ones. Although usually the territories allocated to part-timers are smaller than those given to full-timers, the part-timer isn't under pressure to earn his entire livelihood in direct sales, and this is in his favor, as he can avoid time-wasting parts of his territory.

If you're thinking of going into this field, check it out first. Get answers to these questions:

How much must you invest when starting?

Will it be part-time or full-time?

Will you have to sign a contract, or will it be an informal arrangement?

Will you have to give your Social Security number?

If part-time, will your service dealer accept your customers' checks as payment? This is very important, because it enables you to "launder" the checks, avoiding leaving a paperwork trail.

How much volume does he expect from you?

How good is the territory? You often don't know the answer until you're in it for some weeks, as the dealer will never tell you, "It's a lousy territory."

Why is the dealer not working the territory himself? Sometimes it's simply that it's a bad territory, and not worth his time. In other instances, the dealer prefers to accept a lower income in exchange for more free time, and parcels out parts of his territory to part-timers and collects only the over-ride on their sales. Generally, the dealer will save the best parts for himself. You can be sure of that.

Are you the salesman type? Some people take very well to sales, and seem to have a natural ability for it. Others feel uncomfortable in this role, and don't relate well to strangers. This is a question you must answer honestly, at least to yourself. It might be that, if you're not really suited to sales, you should seek other part-time work.

Can you earn a worthwhile amount by selling to friends, relatives, and fellow employees?

You won't be able to answer all these questions at first. You'll have to play some of it by ear, and judge whether or not it's worth the gamble. Just keep in mind that in direct sales, as in any other field, nobody gives anything away.

NOTES

1. Personal experience of the author, who was one of those salesmen who listened quietly.

21

Barter and Hobbies

BARTER — A QUICK LOOK

Barter is the classic way to earn wealth. Barter existed before money. I've already dealt with barter in a previous book[1] so here I'll just cover a couple of special points.

As your main purpose will be to earn tax-free income, don't follow the popular advice and join a barter exchange. Joining a barter exchange can lead to disaster for the undergrounder.

Normally, individuals and businesses barter services or products in what's come to be known as a "trade-out," in which goods or services are exchanged at a mutually agreeable rate with no money changing hands. The IRS considers barter a form of income, and requires businesses to list their barter income as if it were cash income, based on the "reasonable and customary" price of the goods or services exchanged.

Large businesses can't hide their trade-outs. They often come to millions of dollars, and are impossible to hide, even with the most "creative" accounting methods.

Individuals, because of their limited contacts, may be tempted to join a barter exchange. Contacts are the basic framework of bartering, because you, as someone who has something to trade, need to find another who wants what you have and who has something that you want in return.

How do barter clubs work? You join, and provide information as to what you have to offer. There's a fee for membership, and your name goes on a list, which may or may not be published. Publication of the list is irrelevant, but the existence of the list is all-important, for two reasons.

(1) The IRS has not yet, but may at any time, crack down on barter clubs. In preparation for this, it may be running an "intelligence-gathering" operation to find out the names of members, as they'll all be liable for back taxes and perhaps prosecution. One easy way to do this is to recruit an employee of a barter club to provide a membership list. This is easier to do than many people might think.

An employee who's being audited, and perhaps has some embarrassing back taxes owed, or is even vulnerable to prosecution, is ripe for recruitment. An IRS agent can offer a "deal" (barter, actually), a proposal that all will be forgiven in exchange for the list. This is an offer few can refuse, just as police investigators induce suspects to squeal on fellow-conspirators. If your name is on such a list, it will fall into the hands of the IRS.

A second, and more costly, way is for the IRS to place an undercover agent on the staff of the barter club. The IRS has had undercover agents in the past, and the success of the method suggests they're still using it. This is the alternative if there's nobody already in the barter club's staff that they can suborn.

(2) Membership in such a club can serve as prima facie evidence of intent to evade taxes, if you don't declare your barter income on your return. This will hold up in court, and will leave you in a very uncomfortable position.

BARTER CLUBS — NUTS AND BOLTS

A barter club uses a system of "barter credits," often based on the hours of labor needed to provide goods and services. This can lead to all sorts of disagreements, as some people will feel their labor is undervalued by the club's system.

121

Anyone who provides goods and services "up front" to the club can later feel he's been short-changed. With individual, face-to-face barter, either party can pull out of the deal if he feels he's not getting adequate value, but with the formality of a barter club's rules, this may be difficult or impossible. The dissatisfied individual can demand the return of goods he's provided, but if his trade item is services, and he's already put in the time, recovery is impossible.

With many clubs, there's a system of "barter credits" used as a medium of exchange. This is scrip, certificates that are like money, or perhaps promissory notes. Scrip works like currency, but all the criticisms that apply to currency apply to scrip even more forcefully. Scrip is based on goods and services that often don't yet exist. In that sense, they're like promissory notes, and inflationary. The scrip is no better than the people who back it, and some of these people can be very unreliable.

The cost of membership is variable and tricky. Some clubs charge a flat membership fee. Others tack on a commission for each exchange through the club. Still others may require signing an agreement not to barter except through the club. This is to prevent a person's using the club to make contacts, and then doing extra-curricular trading to avoid paying a commission.

Anyone thinking of joining a barter club should keep in mind one basic fact. The club is a business, like any other business. It exists to make money for the operators. It's wrong to think that it's a group of free spirits dedicated to making life easier for the members. It may, but only in exchange for a fee.

There's yet another danger of membership. In our society, there are many "rip-off" artists, hustlers who live by their wits and try to take unfair advantage of any relationship or opportunity. A rip-off artist who joins a barter club, and then doesn't provide what he's offered, will victimize other members. The club usually collects its fee up front, and has little to lose.

In a face-to-face barter exchange, the people usually know each other, or at least live close by. There is some recourse. If you get shoddy goods from an individual you've contacted through a barter exchange, this person may be halfway across the country. What recourse do you have?

You can always sue. This puts you and your effort in the public record, which it is your purpose to avoid. The value of the goods or services may not be worth a lawsuit, and rip-off artists know this, which is why they get away with many of their games.

Basically, barter clubs have no effective way of policing their members. They can expel a member, but only after the damage is done, and too late for the victims. If you do business through a barter club, you have much to lose.

Face-to-face barter, on the other hand, can be quite safe and rewarding. You usually can trust the other party, because most often you know him.

Direct barter also will be the only way to go in a survival crisis. Whatever happens to the country's money can also happen to barter credits. Cash or goods "on the barrel-head" will be the only rule to follow, and the person who's prepared with a stockpile of trading goods, or a valuable skill, will be in a position to profit.

OPERATING A BARTER-EXCHANGE — THE PITFALLS

This one seems attractive to some, especially those who see themselves as "promoters." Some authorities think it's an appealing prospect.[2]

There are several things wrong with this idea. Let's take the minor ones first. Although this does not require much investment, it does require a lot of time to "set up." If you hold a full-time job, you simply won't have the time.

Another problem is that, like any promotion, it can fall through. There is a high failure rate in any enterprise that deals with services, as much as there is those that deal in products.

Now for the big one. The IRS keeps a close eye on barter exchanges, seeing them as additional sources of information on people who are vulnerable to taxation. Right now, the IRS is not obliging barter exchanges to reveal their records to it, but this could change at any time.[3] If you're the operator of such an exchange, IRS agents could, one fine day, descend on you with a subpoena and force you to open your records to them. Failure or refusal to do so would expose you to prosecution.

At this point, you may be supposing that, if this happens, it's "no skin off your back." It may be so. However, the government sometimes prosecutes people who are only tangentially involved in a crime, and the IRS may regard you as a co-conspirator with the people who evade taxes.

At the very least, you can expect a thorough audit, because as the operator of a barter exchange, the IRS agents will wonder if you have been taking part in some of the transactions, too. This is logical, and in fact you probably would. If you do barter, and don't report it and pay taxes on it, you're in a very exposed position. As the owner and operator of a barter exchange, you're in plain view, and the IRS may decide to do an individual audit, even without examining your operation's records.

This danger is immediate, not in the indefinite future or awaiting the enactment of new laws or regulations. In addition, you're breaking one of the basic "laws" of the underground economy: *Keep a low profile.* As the operator of a barter exchange, you're in the same position as the "Fifth Amendment Taxpayer," waving a red flag in front of the IRS, and expressing open defiance of their efforts by directly supporting and facilitating those who are evading taxes.

The IRS is very vindictive. In their eyes, you're a special "hard case," and they'll give you special attention. In plain language, they'll make you pay.

HOBBIES — MAKING MONEY FROM THEM

Turning a hobby into a money-maker is something many Americans do. Some use their hobbies to earn extra cash in the above-ground economy.

Jack, a bookkeeper for a grocery chain, learned gunsmithing in the army, and repairs guns in his home workshop as a sideline. However, he declares his income, because he has a firearms license from the Federal Government and this makes it impossible to hide the fact that he's running a business. But it doesn't prevent him from skimming cash into his pocket.[4]

Others try to claim their hobbies are businesses, and deduct their hobby expenses on their tax returns.

Jane, who owns two horses, deducted their cost by claiming she was a horse breeder. She got away with it for two years, deducting expenses but not listing any income. The third year an IRS examiner called her in to point out that if she was not making a profit in her business, she ought to get out of business. He informed her that he'd disallow her deductions, as she was not running a bona fide business.[5]

Another way is to work legitimately at money-making with your hobby, enough to use it as a peg upon which you can hang your deductions.

Percy, an accountant, likes photography, and over the years has spent thousands of dollars on equipment. He takes baby pictures on his days off — not many, but enough to show a slight profit, which he declares and uses to justify deducting his equipment and expenses. He has a room in his house set up as a darkroom, and as he uses this room for nothing else, is able to deduct a part of his mortgage, utilities, and telephone bills on his tax form. As an accountant, he knows the Internal Revenue Code better than most, and turns part of it into a loophole for his personal benefit. Thus, his hobby pays, directly and indirectly, for itself and part of his house.

Another way is to use a skill or hobby to earn undeclared income.

"Red" plays the accordian. He works as a printer during the day, but evenings and weekends he plays his instrument for money. His clientele is of two types: the one-shot who hires him to play at weddings, and his regular accounts, including a social club which books him many Friday and Saturday nights.[6]

"Red" accepts payment in cash for most of his work, and signs over the few checks to a second party to cover his tracks. He does not declare his extra income, and thus can't claim any deductions, but he feels that being able to keep all he makes playing on the side more than makes up for the loss of deductions. He's been doing this for fifteen years.

Some take broader views of activities such as hobbies, seeing them as anchors for an alternative economic base. Some even see hobbies as survival skills,[7] very useful in an economic crisis or other arduous situation.

These are but a few examples of people who use their hobbies to help their economic status. There are many hobbies, and many methods of exploiting them.

NOTES

1. *Guerrilla Capitalism,* Adam Cash, Port Townsend, WA, Loompanics Unlimited, 1984, pp. 113-118.

2. *555 Ways To Earn Extra Money,* Jay Conrad Levinson, New York, Holt, Rinehart and Winston, 1982, pp. 292-293.

3. *Guerrilla Capitalism,* p. 111.

4. *Ibid.,* p. 73.

5. *Internal Revenue Code,* Section 182, "Activities Not For Profit." This section defines hobbies and lists the conditions under which an individual may deduct expenses connected with a hobby. Most importantly, it lists what the IRS needs to disallow spurious deductions.

6. *Guerrilla Capitalism,* p. 83.

7. *Government By Emergency,* Dr. Gary North, Fort Worth, TX, American Bureau of Economic Research, 1983, pp. 174-180.

22

Garage Sales

This is usually a way to get rid of your surplus goods,[1] but you can work it into an extra money-maker by a simple device. If you plan to hold a garage sale, do a little brokering on the side. Before you make your preparations, ask your friends and neighbors if they have anything they want to sell.

This is a very efficient way of earning extra money. You have to hold the sale anyway, and pay for a classified ad, put up signs, and lay out your goods in front of your house. It takes a very little additional effort to sell your neighbors' goods, too.

Simply pass the word around, telling your neighbors that they're welcome to sell their goods at your sale. Let them set the prices on what they want to sell. You collect a small commission on every item sold.

The best way to avoid hassles is to follow the rule of letting them set the price very rigidly. The question of how much you collected may come up, and if you haggle with a customer you will sometimes be selling at a price other than what's marked. Having your neighbors decide the prices they want, and marking the items themselves, eliminates all these problems. You'll also save time, which will permit you to negotiate the sales of *your* items.

It's easy to have a "take it or leave it" policy on the items your neighbors leave with you on consignment. If someone wants to discuss anything about the items with you, you can avoid offending them by explaining that the item doesn't belong to you, and that you don't know anything about it except the price that's marked. This cuts the discussion short, and the customer may buy it or move on to something which is yours.

Running a garage or yard sale is not hard to do, if you avoid the simple errors many make.

(1) *Failure to advertise in the classified ads.* These, despite the fine print and the competition from others also advertising garage sales, have a lot of pulling power. More people will see them than will see any signs you may put up. Simply list your sale giving the hours and the address. That's all you really need, and you can save money by avoiding listing all of your goods.

Listing what you have to sell is counter-productive. Garage sales are often impulse-buys, and giving away the information in advance will only keep away potential customers if they decide that they don't want what you have to sell. In any event, you often add last-minute items, which will render any listing obsolete.

(2) *Listing any guns you have to sell.* While it's legal to sell guns, in the states which don't have strict firearms laws, publicizing this risks attracting one or more agents of the Bureau of Alcohol, Tobacco and Firearms. They prowl gun sales, and try to entrap the unwary. There is a kink in the law which makes it illegal to sell a gun to someone who is not a resident of the same state. Often, this is honored in the breach by private sellers, although licensed dealers have to follow the law exactly and ask for ID. BATF agents have posed as customers, trying to buy firearms, and if they were able to buy a gun, they arrested the seller for a violation. The agent making the buy is from out-of-state, and thus has prima facie evidence of the "crime."

If you have guns to sell, put them out on the tables, and have their prices clearly marked. Don't ask for ID, because some of the potential buyers will not want to show it. They're not criminals, but simply gun hobbyists who fear eventual confiscation laws, and want firearms which don't have paper trails leading to them.

This suggests something about pricing these weapons. Gun hobbyists, especially if they're survivalists, are sometimes willing to pay more for a gun which is untraceable. They know that buying from a licensed dealer obliges them to fill out a BATF questionnaire, and to present ID, which Federal agents can use to trace them. They prowl the garage sales with a pocketful of cash, seeking a suitable firearm. The part about cash is necessary for them, and interesting to you. A check leaves a paper trail, and they know that many people will ask for ID before accepting a check, thus the cash.

(3) *Failure to make readable signs.* Many people place signs, despite having advertised in the newspaper, because they seek impulse buyers who are casually driving by. The signs also confirm that there is a sale, and many classified ad readers will look for them. Another reason is that many addresses are not on main streets, and the signs can give directions to the sales. These can simply be arrows.

Many people holding garage sales print their signs on shopping bags, or brown cardboard, which makes them hard to read. Some write too small, trying to crowd as much information as they can onto the sign. They don't stop to realize that most people who read them are motorists, who have to watch the road and can't scrutinize the signs closely. The signs must give the vital information in one glance: "GARAGE SALE" and the address. That's it.

(4) *Failure to have the prices marked on each item.* Some sellers, imagining themselves to be clever negotiators, don't mark their prices. Others are just lazy. This may work in an Arab market, but it just doesn't go in America. Americans

are used to having prices clearly marked, and not having prices visible will simply turn off a number of potential buyers.

Not marking prices brings another problem. You'll be wasting a lot of time answering people who just want to know the prices. This takes you away from the business of closing sales and collecting money. Having a long line will deter people from asking, or buying, and if you have to give verbal prices to a line of people, you'll turn away potential buyers.

Price marking is controversial. There are some who think that not marking prices is the way to separate the buyers from the lookers. This is nonsense. It doesn't hurt you if people look. They still may buy, especially if the prices are attractive. Marking the prices is a service to those who are too shy to ask.

(5) *Failure to understand the value of the items for sale.* Some people have items, such as old sewing machines and other antiques that have been gathering dust for years. They put them up for sale, not realizing that these items can command far higher prices than they ask. There are many antique dealers and collectors who prowl garage sales like a pack of hungry wolves, seeking to buy antiques cheaply from people who don't realize their value. They'll snap up any bargain, and some even have the nerve to try to negotiate the already low price further down.

That's why, if you have any such potential antiques, it's good to know what they're worth. You don't have to be an expert. The way to find out is to go to an antique shop and try to find a similar item, and note the price. If you can't find it, ask the shopkeeper.

One way to ask is to say that you're looking for such an item to complete your collection, and then ask him how much he'd charge you if he had one. You can then calculate that his buying price would be between twenty and fifty percent of his asking price.

A more straightforward way is to tell him outright what you have, and ask him what he'd pay you for it. This is straightforward for you, but not necessarily for him. He may size you up as a person to victimize, and offer you an unrealistically low figure. You can check this out by asking several dealers, or making the rounds. You may find the item on sale in another store, for fifty times the price the first dealer offered. This gives you a clue that he tried to rip you off.

All told, a garage sale is what you make it. It is an opportunity to clear your home of surplus goods, and also a chance to earn extra money, more than you would have gotten normally. Best of all, it's tax-free!

NOTES

1. *On Your Own,* Kathy Matthews, New York, Random House, 1977, pp. 95-96.

23

Temporary Cash Jobs

Andy was between jobs, temporarily out of work while waiting for another job to open up. He knew he'd be back to work in a couple weeks, and also knew the state unemployment office, with its complicated rules and massive bureaucracy, would oblige him to spend several hours of his time traveling to their office, filling out forms, reporting for interviews, and generally wasting his time. He also knew that, with the mandatory one-week waiting period, he'd hardly collect anything for his efforts. Consequently, he didn't bother applying for unemployment benefits.

Instead, he went to an employment agency that specialized in temporary low-grade help, and got a one-day job as a delivery man that very morning. He found that he had to pay the fee, ten percent, in advance, but that the employer paid him for eight hours' work even though he worked only six. The next morning, he went back to the same employment agency and got a one-day job for a different company. The next morning, he got a day's work delivering for a third company. To his surprise, all paid him in cash, not checks. The pay was minimum wage, but eight hours' pay and no taxes meant that in reality he earned more than minimum.

The drawback was that ten-percent agency fee, up front. It was like a tax, but still lower than the Federal Government's current fourteen percent base rate. The work was not too unpleasant, and as a temporary employee he simply did his job and went home at the end of the day with no hassle and no worries about company politics. Within a couple of weeks, the job he'd been awaiting opened up for him. He felt as if he'd been on vacation for several weeks, although he'd earned money almost every day.

Temporary employees are privileged. In some instances, they earn more than permanent staff.

Mickey was an electronics engineer, "job-shopping." This means that he worked for a temporary agency, not the company. His terms of employment never lasted more than four months, but his hourly wage was higher than that of the permanent engineers. As a temporary, he was on hourly, not salary, and got paid for overtime, too. The regular staff did not. This was not underground work at all, as he had to pay taxes on his income. But after several years and experience at many different companies, he put the word out that he was available as a free-lancer. That meant he'd work temporarily, but charge a lower rate than the agency would charge the company, as the agency had to mark up his pay to make a profit. He asked for payment in cash, and a few employers agreed. With the others, he laundered his checks. In effect, he set himself up in competition with the agency that provided him with temporary jobs, secure in the knowledge that he had enough private accounts not to be hurt if they found out and stopped dealing with him.

This is very much like contract labor, with all the opportunities for earning more money than working at a conventional job and of keeping more of it. In some fields, it's lucrative. Some of the fields in which it's worthwhile are nursing, engineering, construction, casual labor, and general office work. One field in which it doesn't work as well is teaching. While there are many substitute teachers, filling in for special classes or when regular teachers call in sick, schools are highly-structured, and very prissy about cooperating with an undergrounder and paying cash. It's necessary to have a way of laundering all the income, which might not be possible.

Those who can best get away with temporary work are those with other ostensible means of support, such as housewives. With the husband as the declared wage-earner, the housewife can sell her time and skills without causing a ripple and attracting investigation. There are many housewives who gave up lucrative careers upon marriage, and who are still Registered Nurses and licensed teachers.

Arlene was a Registered Nurse, married to an insurance agent. She was listed with an agency that provided temporary medical staff. Her two children were old enough to be "latchkey children" on the days when she got calls. When she filled in at hospitals, she declared her income. Some days, however, she filled in at doctors' private offices, and sometimes the doctor, himself hiding part of his income, would sympathetically pay her cash. She also developed a clientele among a few doctors who were pleased with her work, and who would call her at home when they needed her instead of going through the agency. This enabled her to avoid the paperwork trail that would betray her if ever there was an audit and investigation.

The final word about temporary work is that it can be very pleasant indeed. If you're a temporary, you're not involved in office or shop politics. The other employees don't worry about your angling for their jobs, or for a promotion. When you go home, you can relax. Even a high-pressure environment is not as bad as it is for the people who have to look forward to it for many more months or years. If you find a workplace you don't like for any reason, you can simply refuse to go back, as there are other openings available.

24

Street Trades

This very loose term applies to all sorts of street businesses, mostly involving selling products or services. The street trader is mobile, and may overlap with or duplicate the businessman who operates from a fixed location.

Some examples are: pushcart peddlers of all sorts, including frankfurter stands or carts, ice cream vendors, peanut vendors, etc.; mobile photographic "studios," with which the vendor takes snapshots of clients, develops, prints, and sells them on the spot; street artists who draw portraits, caricatures, and profiles of clients on the spot, working with paper, canvas, or engraving them onto copper plates.

The forms which this sort of business can take are quite varied. Some enterprisers are simply peddlers, operating out of suitcases and setting up on well-traveled corners. In some Western cities, street-corner flower sellers operate with a basket of flowers, selling bouquets to passing motorists. In cities with a lot of pedestrians, street-corner peddlers sell wind-up toys, small notions and articles of clothing, and other light, durable goods.

Others have more elaborate set-ups, such as carts or even trucks in the case of ice-cream vendors. An investment in equipment is necessary for a seller of frankfurters or ice cream.

The operator of a "newsstand," selling newspapers, magazines, candy and tobacco, differs from the store owner only in that he uses a wooden or metal shack erected on a sidewalk instead of renting a store. His premises are more austere, usually lacking some physical comforts such as heating, running water, and a toilet, and because of limited space he can't carry much stock. On the other hand, he can do as much business as a store owner, or even more if he has a good location, and he keeps more of the earnings because his overhead is lower.

Opening up a street business is not a formula for guaranteed success, especially for the Guerrilla Capitalist. The big advantage is that, because of the nature of the business and the small value of the items, he deals mainly in cash, but there are many disadvantages that can go with it.

One is that, in many cities, the street vendor needs a license, either a "peddler's" license or a business and sales tax license. This immediately creates a paperwork trail, an entry on a list which the tax authorities scan regularly to ensure they're collecting from all who are in business.

Tax collectors are aware that businesses which deal mainly in cash are hard to audit, and they pay special attention to them.

Despite this, there are many underground street vendors who operate in jurisdictions that require licenses, avoiding the paperwork by not operating from fixed locations, but they're highly mobile, working out of suitcases and ready to move on when necessary. They keep a watch for approaching policemen, and can pack up and melt into the crowd on a moment's notice.

In some locales, law enforcement is strict, with the police handing out summonses to illegal vendors. In practice, it's hard to enforce such ordinances, because some of these vendors have literally no fixed addresses, or at least don't give them to the police. As most of these operate on foot, they don't need driver's licenses, and in fact many residents of Eastern cities with good public transport don't have driver's licenses and don't own cars. With recent Supreme Court decisions making "vagrancy" laws unconstitutional, there's little a police officer can do about people who don't show "ID" when asked, unless they're suspects in major crimes.

In many larger cities, whatever the laws may be regarding street sales, the police have enough to do without concerning themselves with minor offenses. With high rates of major "street crimes," some police forces have even adopted policies of not enforcing laws pertaining to "victimless crimes," such as prostitution (a classic street trade) and gambling. With such policies, we can see that street peddlers are very low on a police department's list of priorities.

In other cities, where the local police follow a tradition of graft, the street vendor avoids hassles with the law by paying off the local beat cop, and considers this a normal business expense.

Another disadvantage is that some enterprises, such as selling ice cream, frankfurters, and other foods requires a license from the Board of Health in many jurisdictions. This is an additional expense, and lays a paperwork trail.

In some cases, such as that of a street artist who sets up shop at a public event, there's an opportunity to earn a lot of money in a very short time. Often, especially if the event is one with controlled access, such as a state fair, he might need a temporary license or permit from the managers of the fair. They may or may not require proof of identity, but usually are only interested in collecting the fees. This means the Guerrilla Capitalist can surface for a day or two, do his business, and submerge into the depths once he's finished.

The opportunities for street vendors vary widely with the locale, as we've seen, and it's hard to generalize because there are so many special situations.

25

Opportunities for Children

Child labor practices have changed over the years. Originally, children were economic assets. Today, parents must support them while they're in school, until they "come of age." In an agricultural society, they were able to help out on the farm from before puberty, boosting the family's economy. The industrial era changed all that, as more people gave up farming and moved to the cities. Child exploitation in unhealthy factories was one of the unpleasant features of Nineteenth Century American life.

The turn of the century saw the passage of comprehensive child-labor laws to protect young people against economic exploitation. The effect of these laws generally was good, because there was an increasing need for education to enable a young person to hold his own in the marketplace, where jobs increasingly demanded higher levels of skill and education. Restricting the employment of children thus assisted the programs of the public schools that provided children with minimal educations to give them a start in the adult labor market.

For most of this century, children have been barred from the labor market, with certain exceptions. School-age children have, with government permission, been able to work at certain part-time jobs which did not interfere with their educations.

Ambitious young people, however, are not totally unable to earn money except with the government's permission. Only salaried labor is controlled. "Working papers" apply only to formal employment on a regular basis with established businesses. These keep records, withhold taxes, and comply with all of the licensing requirements of the local jurisdiction.

Those wishing to strike out on their own find that young people have special status in the eyes of the law. As a start, the problem of income taxes often doesn't apply to them. The Internal Revenue Code exempts people below a certain level of income from even filing returns, for example. They legally remain in the underground economy.

Another advantage is a practical exemption from licensing requirements and keeping records. While local health officials enforce the health code with restaurants, a kid selling lemonade on the corner won't have to cope with this hassle. A child running a business also won't find city or state tax collectors hassling him regarding sales taxes or business permits.

Another advantage is an almost total immunity from prosecution. Normally, even violations of the criminal code apply less severely to someone who's "under-age." In the case of a technical infraction of licensing requirements, or some provisions of the Internal Revenue Code, the young person's very unlikely to wind up in court, as any prosecutor would appear silly coming down hard on a young and minor offender when there are so many mature and flagrant ones unprosecuted.

ADVANTAGES

Apart from the law, children have certain advantages over adults in the business world. This results not only from their status as minors, but because most of them live with their parents.

(1) They're under little or no pressure to "get a job," as are adults. They don't have bills to pay, food to buy, and all the other burdens adults carry. This gives them the freedom to take their time, select carefully, and not rush into something just because "it's a job and I've got bills to pay."

(2) Not being under pressure, they have more freedom to decide that they've made a mistake and give up, if an enterprise turns sour. Although Americans like to say they don't give up, and they despise "quitters," abandoning an unprofitable pursuit makes more sense than perservering in an unhealthy or unprofitable situation.

This is especially important in the case of children. Expecting someone to decide on a career at an early age is unreasonable. Immature people often don't know themselves and their abilities well enough to predict how well they'll do in an occupation. With no work experience, young persons often can't know how they'll make out in a short-term pursuit, and the freedom to make a change is vital.

(3) Children, living at home and usually seeking ways to earn money simply to enhance their allowances, don't have the overheads that mature businessmen carry. They don't have to make a certain volume of business per month to keep their heads above water, and they don't have to make heavy investments to permit this. Not having a minimum volume, and not having to cope with overhead, they have the freedom to work at almost whatever level of effort they wish. This is very important for the school-age child, who is serious about his academic work and doesn't want to compromise his chances for an adult career by neglecting his studies.

(4) Minimal investment is the common factor among businesses that young people start. Because young people simply don't have the money, they tend towards enterprises they can start on a shoe-string, and fortunately there are many of these, giving the beginner a wide choice. In many instances the employer furnishes the tools and equipment,

141

such as in mowing lawns. In others, they can get help from their families.

(5) For a young person, a money-making pursuit is the first step towards independence, which many crave. Depending on an allowance is not very satisfying. Earning money independently gives the youngster the emotional fulfilment of not being beholden to parents in this regard.

AVOIDING TRAPS

One of the hard facts of life is that, no matter how many laws there are, and how rigorously they're enforced, some of the sharpest minds in the country will be working to circumvent them. Child exploitation is still with us, but in various guises.

One excellent example is that of newspaper carriers. Newspaper circulation managers, always seeking cheap labor to deliver their papers to subscribers, use a loop-hole in the law to exploit children. The practice varies from state to state, and certainly in some states delivering newspapers can be worthwhile. In others, it's "the pits."

For the young person contemplating this, a good way to tell is by looking at the advertisements in the local paper. If they constantly advertise for newspaper carriers, it means that they have a high turn-over, an unsubtle hint that there's something terrible wrong with the working conditions.

Typically, the carrier is not an employee of the newspaper. He's a contract employee, which means that he gets a certain fee for delivering each copy. In many instances, he's actually a dealer, which in plain language means that he buys the newspapers from the company, delivers them, and is responsible for collecting the subscription money. If he has trouble collecting from an account, the circulation manager isn't interested. That's not his problem, and the child has to cope with it as best he can. Nevertheless, he's responsible for paying his bill to the newspaper each week, to cover the copies he takes to deliver. In climates where weather is inclement, the child has to tough it out, or quit.

Other problems come up, with some newspapers. Some have erratic press runs, which means that although the papers are supposed to come off the press at a certain time each day, they're often late, and the carrier must wait around for them. As he's an independent contractor, he's not paid for this waiting time, which sometimes is as much as three hours.[1] Basically, as the newspaper managers don't pay the carrier for his time, they don't care. This is important when the carrier calculates whether or not he's earning enough money for the time he invests.

The advertisements for carriers that newspapers run claim this is good training in basic business practice for the young entrepreneur, and that the experience he gains will benefit him in later life. This is merely glossing over the fact that he's on his own, and as an independent contractor under these dictated conditions, he usually gets the dirty end of the deal. In one sense, the experience is valuable, because he gains first-hand knowledge of what it's like to be conned and exploited, without the danger of being hurt as badly as he would in adult life.

An additional problem comes from the attitudes that some adults have towards young people. While they expect, and even demand respect from youngsters, they don't reciprocate, and are very obvious in their treatment of them as second-class citizens. They act as if young people have no rights at all, and should be grateful for anything they get. Problem personalities such as these are some of the traps young persons can encounter.

The traps usually follow the same pattern. Usually, they involve reporting for "work" at a certain hour each day at the same place, whether it be a newspaper office or a motion picture theater, having to provide equipment, such as a bicycle or a uniform, and uncertainty regarding the number of hours required. Any young person contemplating such a job should first ask any of his friends who work there about

143

working conditions. This highlights one of the most important principles of job-hunting, both in the juvenile and adult worlds: "Check out the boss as carefully as he checks you out."

STARTING OUT

The simplest way to start is by "hustling," which means knocking on doors. A young person seeking part-time jobs without any of the hassles of filling out applications and possibly letting himself in for traps can hustle his neighborhood, going from door to door and asking if the householder needs any work done. Often, this will produce a "hit" very quickly. Almost everyone needs something done for which they're willing to pay a young person. It may be time to mow the lawn, rake up leaves, clean out a store-room, etc. Many household chores wind up neglected, because the adult doesn't have the time, but more often because it's boring work and he finds excuses for putting it off. This gives the young and ambitious person the opportunity to sell his services on a one-time basis, with the prospect of repeat business if the outcome is satisfactory.

This "take the money and run" practice may seem insecure, as it is somewhat erratic and depends on finding enough people who need odd jobs done each week, but in reality it has certain advantages. The minor doesn't tie himself down to a fixed job, with the problems that it may bring if it's unpleasant. If he doesn't like it, he can finish off the work that afternoon, collect his money, and not return. It's not a long-term commitment.

An advantage of this canvassing is that the youngster is already known in the neighborhood, and doesn't have the problem of presenting himself to a stranger, and filling out applications to lay out his background, which most employers demand.

Another advantage is in collecting for the work. Although taking unfair advantage of a minor is despicable in the eyes of most people, there are some adults who will do it. Some of them simply don't pay, or delay paying. They make excuses, claiming they don't have the money "right now," and tell the minor to come back another day. When he returns, they again plead poverty, hoping that the minor will simply get tired of coming back and leaving him repeatedly frustrated.

Not many people will "stiff" a child, but if the young enterpriser does find one, he avoids getting in too deeply if his work is a one-shot deal, and he can avoid that person in the future. Meanwhile, he'll be earning money from other, more honorable people, and the loss won't hurt as much.

JOBS WITH NO INVESTMENT

Knocking on doors usually means that the employer provides the equipment. A housewife who needs help in cleaning windows won't expect the young person to run home and get his own rags and cleaning fluid. The householder will usually have a rake or lawnmower, and whatever other tools are needed for the work.

There are many tasks for which the young enterpriser can earn money without providing anything but his time and effort. One of these is babysitting, in which the parents supply absolutely everything from baby food to diapers, and often even a meal or snack for the babysitter if the task runs through suppertime.

Similar to babysitting is pet walking, for business couples who feel they don't have the time. Again, the client supplies the dog and the leash, and the young enterpriser furnishes only the labor.

"Wash your car, mister?" is usually the start of another investment-free job. Saturday afternoon is the traditional time to canvass the neighborhood for this sort of work.

In many areas, Wednesday and Friday are the big supermarket shopping days. While many supermarkets include carts and even free carry-out service for people who need help in trundling their loads to their cars, those in the city don't always have parking lots, and shoppers have to make their way home on foot. Young persons who take up posts near the doors of such markets, offering a shopping bag carrying service, can canvass their way to some extra dollars on a busy day.

Laundromats are also sources of extra income. Some housewives need help in stacking the wash, or folding bedsheets.

Washing windows for a harried homemaker is just one service. Housewives may also need help in other ways, such as carpet beating, hanging washing, shoveling snow, and raking leaves. Some need help in their "spring cleaning," which can keep an energetic young person busy all day.

Delivering advertising materials is similar to running a newspaper route, but it's usually a one-shot. This is both good and bad. The disadvantage is that it's not steady work. The advantages are that there's usually no time lost waiting for the material to be printed, no customer complaints for missing a house, and no need to collect money. Payment may be by the hour, or by a fixed fee for every thousand delivered.

SCROUNGING BRASS

Anyone living in an area where the shooting sports are popular can spend a day walking through the informal shooting areas, picking up empty cases. Rifle ranges have strict rules, and don't offer much opportunity to pick up brass. Many people, however, go shooting against hillsides, and those who don't reload their shells often leave them where they fall. These are worth at least three to five cents each to a gun hobbyist, and it's often possible to find dozens in one place, and sometimes even the box. Spotting a shooting area from far off is easy. Usually, it's up against a hill or berm, and there's a clear area where the bullets fall and destroy the greenery. Often, shooters leave cans and bottles behind them when they go home.

Walking the field up to one hundred yards from the impact area will give the best chance for finding brass. Close-in, there's pistol brass, such as .38 Special, .357 Magnum, and 9mm Luger. Many rifle shooters also fire at close ranges, and rifle brass is commonly available, too.

Certain times are better than others for finding brass. Many people shoot on weekends, and walking a shooting area just after the shooters leave gives a good chance to find their leavings. The start of hunting season produces a crop of rifle brass, as the hunters come out to sight in their rifles. The few days after Christmas are also worthwhile, because the "Christmas Gun" offers an irresistable temptation to go into the field to try it out quickly. Many who give guns for Christmas also include a box or two of ammunition, and if they don't the new gun is an irresistible incentive to buy a couple of boxes to enable shooting it. If the shooter is not a reloader, the chances are that he'll leave his brass.

The .22 shells are not reloadable, but it's possible to recycle them for the brass and sell them to a smelter. However, they're so light that it's necessary to pick up very many of them to get a signficant amount of money, and most don't bother.

All center-fire brass is worth picking up, even if it's tarnished. Reloaders have ways of cleaning them up and restoring the factory shine. Any shells that are crushed, creased, or cracked are damaged, and not worth the trouble. Otherwise, anything goes.

It's easy to find buyers for the popular calibers. In pistol, there are .38 Special, .357 Magnum, 9mm Luger, and .45 ACP. Popular rifle calibers are .30-30, .223, .308, and 30-06. The less commonly-used calibers are harder to sell, but a good outlet is a gun shop. Many normally carry fired brass to sell to reloaders, and the managers are willing to buy brass from anyone who brings it in. Although the gun store must make a profit, the brass scrounger can expect a good price for the rare calibers, because the store charges more for them.

INVESTMENT FOR MONEY-MAKING

There are some tasks that require small investments. The young person may be able to beg or borrow the equipment, or he may have to buy it himself. Parents are often willing to let a young enterpriser use the family lawnmower for working a "route," and anyone offering a window-cleaning service on a regular basis instead of casually can start by scrounging rags and cleaning fluid from his household, replenishing the supply with the money he earns.

Sometimes it takes actual "seed money." In one instance, a boy who got a job delivering telegrams after school persuaded his mother to buy him a bicycle for the task. Relatives often will lay out interest-free loans or an outright gift for the capitalization of the business.

Canvassing the neighborhood, offering a lawn-mowing service, or leaf raking, makes a better impression if the young businessman has the equipment, a rake or lawnmower with him. Trimming hedges likewise requires a special tool, a hedge trimmer, and the one who has the trimmer in his hand and can go to work immediately has an advantage over the one for whom the homeowner must get out the tools. In cold climates, a youngster with his own shovel can pick up work by ringing doorbells after a snowfall.

Shining shoes used to be a popular occupation for young people, but lately, with the increased informality in dress, and the widespread wearing of running shoes, there's simply less shoe-leather to polish. In some areas, such as a downtown business district, a boy with a shoe-shine box may be able to pick up a few bucks catering to the three-piece-suit trade. The minimal investment includes the box, rags, shoe wax, and a couple of brushes.

Selling soft drinks at a public event also requires a minimal investment. Paper cups, ice, and the fixings for lemonade or whatever flavor sells best are the minimum needed. Selling to construction crews on hot days can also be worth the time and trouble, unless they're all devoted to beer.

Recycling in various forms requires a slight investment. This can be on the family level, collecting soda and beer cans, stomping them flat, and periodically persuading a relative to help transport them to a recycling center. This only requires paper or plastic bags to hold the cans.

On a slightly higher level, the young person can seek recyclables from friends and neighbors. Newspapers and magazines go to paper recycling firms. Metals of various sorts sell, depending on the metal and its application. If the young person can scrounge used wheel weights from local garages, he can sell them to gun hobbyists who cast their own bullets. Most gas stations do save their wheel weights for specific outlets, and finding any willing to give them away is becoming increasingly difficult.

An ambitious young person can start a "route" buying or building a cart and making the rounds each afternoon, looking for throw-aways. Newspapers and rags are the traditional recyclables, but aluminum cans have become popular and lucrative during the last decade.

One of the symptoms of an affluent society is conspicuous waste. People throw away items that are still useful, sometimes just because they're several years old and they've bought a new one. Many of these throw-aways are worth picking up. Some are appliances, including TV sets, that need only minor repairs to make them serviceable. Collecting these and selling them to a second-hand store can bring extra dollars.

In many instances, it's possible to salvage parts from an appliance that's not working. Washers and dryers all have electric motors, and most of them are in running condition. Some repair men strip down old appliances for the parts, which they can install on their own work. Many cities have "stop and swap" second-hand stores that deal exclusively in salvaged material.

Not surprisingly, it's possible to pick up enough serviceable material from people's garbage to start a garage sale. Among the items people throw out are: clothing, cassette tapes, records, books, hand tools, toys, flashlights, kitchen utensils, and ashtrays. This is a very short and incomplete list, but it shows the range of material available. The only investment required is a cart to haul it away.

KEEPING IT ALL

Most people pay kids in cash. They know that youngsters don't have checking accounts, and don't take Master Charge. This means clean income, utterly invisible, and in any event most young people don't earn enough even to have to file. This means that they are, for all practical purposes, exempt from the tax bite. Starting out in business young is starting out the right way — in the underground economy. The experience will be valuable later.

NOTES

1. One newspaper for which the author worked had a chronic problem with press runs, for various reasons, and a horde of carriers had to wait at the pressroom gate often for hours each day. At this newspaper, the carriers typically had to wait over an hour to pick up bundles that typically took only an hour to deliver.

26

The IRS, Big Brother
and the Guerrilla Capitalist

In 1984, IRS Commissioner Roscoe Egger approved a "Strategic Plan to carry out the Mission of the Service." Contained in Document 6941 (5-84), this Strategic Plan included a blueprint for combatting tax evasion. The IRS needed such a blueprint because of "a continuing decline in the extent to which taxpayers are willing or able to comply with federal tax laws."[1] Document 6941 attributed this decline to a number of "significant trend factors," including changes in attitudes toward authority.

On this point, the document said, "Taxpayers are exhibiting a declining respect for and reliance on 'the law' and government in general. A 'decay in the social contract' is detectable; there is a growing feeling, particularly among middle-income taxpayers, that they are not getting back, from society and government, their money's worth for taxes paid. The tendency is for taxpayers to try to take more control of their finances, perhaps because they see an uncertain economic future for themselves; they exhibit a declining willingness to pay the share of governmental expenditures (including expenditures they may strongly disagree with) which government says is theirs to pay."[2]

Document 6941 also cited changes in tax avoidance "sophistication" as a contributing factor. "Taxpayers are becoming better informed about the existence of tax abuses (tax shelters and the like), the extend of tax cheating (the 'tax gap' has been widely publicized), and the difficulty for government to detect and deal with tax abuses. Consequently, taxpayers in general are becoming more inclined to avoid and evade taxes through such means as are available to them."[3]

Of course, none of this should be news to readers of these Guerrilla Capitalism volumes, since we've previously pointed out these same developments. However, it is interesting to hear our analysis echoed by the revenuers themselves.

But the question is: What is the IRS doing to fight these developments" And more importantly: How effective are its efforts?

The Strategic Plan included fifteen specific initiatives to be pursued, aimed at "strengthening voluntary compliance." Some of these initiatives are far from frightening, such as the proposal to "heighten awareness of tax cheating consequences," particularly by "publicizing information about the many enforcement sanctions available to the Service."[4] Since few, if any, Guerrilla Capitalists are unaware of the IRS's "many enforcement sanctions," such fear propaganda is not likely to have much effect.

Some of the initiatives included in the Strategic Plan may be of some usefulness to the revenuers. For example, the proposal to develop a "three-year taxpayer profile" including information not shown on tax returns. This is supposed to supplement the Discriminate Function (DIF) in selecting returns for auditing and to aid tax examiners during the auditing process. However, since the IRS is auditing fewer returns than ever, about 12 out of every 1,000,[5] the usefulness of this initiative is obviously limited. Of course, some categories of returns are more likely to be audited than the overall average. Schedule C (unincorporated business) filers face an audit risk of one chance in fifteen.[6] Those are still fairly good odds for the Guerrilla Capitalist.

152

The IRS Strategic Plan also included a proposal to "develop additional sources of information to detect noncompliance through cooperative programs with the states."[7] But the IRS already receives data from employers, banks and states for computer-matching with tax returns to catch "cheaters." And it does not even use all the information it now receives. Thus, the IRS simply did not use 22% of the records it received for the 1983 tax year.[8] Furthermore, about 40% of the cases of suspected tax evasion turned up by its computer-matching efforts are simply dropped for lack of staff.[9] If the IRS can't use all the information it is already receiving, how much good will additional information do the revenuers?

The Strategic Plan expressed particular concern about the problem of noncompliance among the self-employed, whose numbers are increasing. The Plan called for a "Returns Compliance Project" to identify self-employed nonfilers. "This can be accomplished by selecting a random sample of commercial lists of individuals who have high incomes but who are not shown on the Individual Master File (IMF) or otherwise identified through the Information Returns Program (IRP). (This project would be separate from the Commercial List 'test' being run in selected districts)"[10]

The last sentence refers to a project, begun in February, 1984, to identify nonfilers in four test areas: Brooklyn, Indianapolis, Milwaukee and Reno, Nevada. From a private company, the IRS purchased a list of households estimated to have incomes of $10,000 or more. The income estimates are based on information about real estate transactions, automobile registrations, magazine subscriptions, etc.[11] So far, we've seen no reports on the effectiveness of this test project. In any case, the project is aimed at identifying self-employed *nonfilers*, who probably constitute a very small minority among Guerrilla Capitalists. So very few are likely to be caught in this net.

Although the IRS's 1984 Strategic Plan has some ominously Orwellian aspects, such as the expressed intention to "seek additional ways to create and maintain a sense of presence"[12], remember that the best-laid plans of mice and men go oft astray. Indeed, despite the grand Strategic Plan adopted in 1984, 1985 proved to be a particularly bad year for the IRS.

In at least one case in 1985, IRS employees simply shredded thousands of tax returns without entering them into the records or crediting the taxpayers. In some centers, unprocessed documents clogged hallways to such an extent that fire marshals were called in to clean out the mess. There were constant breakdowns of the computer systems because the untrained personnel didn't know how to operate even the simplest of them. The chaos was at its peak in the Philadelphia office, where hundreds of thousands of returns were lost, mislaid or destroyed.[13]

Although things went more smoothly for the revenuers in 1986, there were still some mishaps. Thus, it was reported that the IRS lost, misplaced or accidently erased 58 reels of computer tape containing records of interest and dividend income for 1983.[14]

Obviously, the revenuers are not ten feet tall. They have a few strengths and a great many limitations. As the IRS itself admitted in Document 6941, one reason for the growth of the underground economy is that people are becoming better informed about the difficulty for the government to detect and deal with tax evasion. The Guerrilla Capitalist who takes advantage of the IRS's weakness, while keeping a low profile and avoiding a dangerous confrontation, can earn extra money in the underground economy and keep what he earns.

NOTES

1. *Internal Revenue Service Strategic Plan.* Document 6941 (5-84), Internal Revenue Service, p. 45.

2. *Ibid.*

3. *Ibid.*

4. *Ibid.,* p. 55.

5. "What's Hot In Taxes This Year?" by Paul N. Strassels, *Dollars & Sense,* May 1986, p. 10.

6. *Ibid.*

7. *Internal Revenue Service Strategic Plan,* p. 67.

8. "IRS' cheaters search falling billions short," by Marilyn Adams, *USA Today.* (The clipping I have is not dated, but the contents of the article indicate that it was published in 1986.)

9. *Ibid.*

10. *Internal Revenue Service Strategic Plan,* p. 75.

11. "IRS sifts mail lists for cheats," by William Giese, *USA Today.* (Undated clipping.)

12. *Internal Revenue Service Strategic Plan,* p. 47.

13. "IRS in Disarry," by Martin Larson, *The Spotlight.* (Undated clipping.)

14. "IRS' cheaters search falling billions short," by Marilyn Adams, *USA Today.*

27

Recommended Reading

This continues the "Recommended Reading" lists in *GUERRILLA CAPITALISM* and *HOW TO DO BUSINESS "OFF THE BOOKS."*

THE UNDERGROUND ECONOMY

How To Do Business "Off The Books," by Adam Cash. 1986, Loompanics Unlimited, Port Townsend, WA 98368. The second volume of my trilogy on Guerrilla Capitalism.

The Organization of Illegal Markets: An Economic Analysis, by Peter Reuter. 1986, Loompanics Unlimited, Port Townsend, WA. Scholarly analysis of illegal businesses and how they are organized.

THE IRS, TAXES, AND FIDDLING THE BOOKS

The Great Income Tax Hoax, by Irwin Schiff. 1984, Freedom Books, PO Box 5303, Hamden, CT 06518. Points out, among other things, that the 16th Amendment (Income Tax Amendment) was never properly ratified by the States, and that the income tax is null and void.

Hit Back At The I.R.S., by Ragnar the Avenger. 1986, The Technology Group, PO Box 93124, Pasadena, CA 91109. Hard-core guerrilla war against the IRS, includes how to get the home addresses of IRS agents.

Illegal Tax Protestor Information Book. Secret report for IRS agents, which is actually a "hit list" prepared by the IRS's Criminal Investigation Office of Intelligence. The IRS ordered all copies of the report destroyed. Available from Liberty Library, 300 Independence Ave SE, Washington, DC 20003.

Internal Revenue Service Strategic Plan. IRS Document 6941 (5-84). The official IRS plan to ferret out Guerrilla Capitalists.

Screw The I.R.S. A card game. 1984, Century Game Co., PO Box 290125, St. Louis, MO 63129. A fun game for the whole family. This company also sells "Screw The I.R.S." coffee mugs, buttons, and stickers.

To Harass Our People: The IRS and Government Abuse of Power, by George Hansen. 1984, Positive Publications, Box 23560, Washington, DC 20024. Good expose of fascist IRS methods, written by an ex-Congressman who was and is the target of IRS harassment.

Twelve Deadly Negatrends, by Dr. Gary North. 1985, American Bureau of Economic Research, PO Box 8204, Fort Worth, TX 76124. North is one of the better conservative and hard-money writers.

STARTING NEW BUSINESSES AND MOONLIGHTING

Cash From Square Foot Gardening, by Mel Bartholomew. 1985, Storey Publishing, Pownal, VT 05261. An excellent book on gardening as a part-time business, with emphasis on how to get paid in cash.

555 Ways To Earn Extra Money, by Jay Conrad Levinson. 1982, Holt, Rinehart, and Winston. Ideas for earning extra money.

How To Collect Unemployment Insurance (Even If You're Not Eligible),, by H.R.D. 1981, Loompanics Unlimited, Port Townsend, WA. Many Guerrilla Capitalists collect unemployment while moonlighting off the books.

How To Convert Your Favorite Hobby, Sport, Pastime Or Idea To Cash, by Al Riolo. 1983, Business Development and Research Center, PO Box 5499, Sacramento, CA 95817. Good book on making a business of your hobby. Very well thought out.

How To Make Money As A Process Server, by Ralph D. Thomas. 1985, Thomas Publications, Austin, TX. A sideline business that can be run on a cash basis.

How To Sell Your Homemade Creation, by Allan H. Smith. 1985, Success Publishing, 8084 Nashua Driver, Lake Park, FL 33410. Selling home crafts in today's marketplace.

Make Money In Diving, by Jon-Paul Giguere. 1981, Rave Publications, 3906 N 69th St, Milwaukee, WI 53216. Many different ways of making money underwater.

The #1 Home Business Book, by George and Sandra Delany. 1981, Liberty Publishing Company, Cockeysville, MD. How to start a business in your home.

On Your Own, by Kathy Matthews. 1977, Random House, New York. Alternatives to a 9-to-5 job.

Over 325 Ways To Make Money While Living In The Country, by Bill Camp. 1985, BC Studios, Box 5908, Huntington Beach, CA 92615. Rural money-making.

Sewing For Profits, by Judith and Allan Smith. 1985, Success Advertising and Publishing, 8084 Nashua Drive, Lake Park, FL 33408. How to start a home sewing business.

Temporary Employment: The Flexible Alternative, by Demaris C. Smith. 1985, Betterway Publications, White Hall, VA. All about temporary employment, from both employee and employer points of view.

Treasure Hunting: A Modern Search for Adventure, by H. Glenn Carson. 1973, Carson Enterprises Ltd. 801 Juniper Ave., Boulder, CO 80302. How to find all sorts of lost stuff, both with and without a metal detector.

"UNDERGROUND" INVESTING

Alternative Americas, by Mildred J. Loomis. 1982, Universe Books, 381 Park Ave South, New York, NY 10016. A classic book on political decentralization.

The Best Investment: Land in a Loving Community, by David W. Felder. 1982, Wellington Press, PO Box 13504, Tallahassee, FL 32308. Advocates moving to a rural community as a good investment.

Cut Your Electric Bills In Half, by Ralph J. Herbert. 1986, Rodale Press, Emmaus, PA. A penny saved is more than a penny earned.

Ecotopian Encyclopedia, by Ernest Callenbach. 1981, And/Or Press, Berkeley, CA. Full of ideas on how to save money.

Gene Logsdon's Money-Saving Secrets: A Treasure of Salvaging, Bargaining, Recycling & Scavenging Techniques, by Gene Logsdon. 1986, Rodale Press, Emmaus, PA. Good tips on saving money — remember a penny saved is better than a penny earned.

Getting A Roof Over Your Head, compiled by the Garden Way editors. 1983, Garden Way Publishing, Charlotte, VT 05445. Affordable housing alternatives.

Home Food Systems, edited by Roger B. Yepsen, Jr. 1981, Rodale Press, Emmaus, PA. How to produce, process, and preserve your own food.

BARTER

How To Get On The Barter Bandwagon, by Mark E. Fournier. 1980, Phoenix Books, PO Box 32008, Phoenix, AZ 85064. Beginner's book on barter.

Survival Bartering, by Duncan Long. 1986, Loompanics Unlimited. How to barter, with emphasis on survival situations.

PRIVACY AND DODGING BIG BROTHER

Liar's Manual, by Roland Baker. 1983, Nelson-Hall, Chicago. A how-to-do-it manual on telling lies. Might be useful to Guerrilla Capitalists.

"Media Research Reports," available from EPIA Society, PO Box 6163, San Bernardino, CA 92412. Many fascinating reports encouraging citizens to resist government licensing of all sorts, including business licenses, marriage licenses, drivers licenses, and birth certificates.

Shadowing And Surveillance, by Burt Rapp. 1986, Loompanics Unlimited, Port Townsend, WA. A how-to-do-it manual on secret surveillance.

Undercover Work, by Burt Rapp. 1986, Loompanics Unlimited, Port Townsend, WA. A revealing look at the nuts-and-bolts of undercover operations.

YOU WILL ALSO WANT TO READ: